OUTBACK ODYSSEY

TRAVELS IN HIDDEN AUSTRALIA

JOHN DWYER

For Grace and Hannah, my inspirations

1

PERTH

Had it not been for that storm, I could have been Australian. Had fate dealt me a different hand, I may well have been a lifeguard on Bondi Beach, bounding across the sand as my tight red shorts and rippling six-pack attracted admiring glances from the ladies. Or else I might have been a hardened Outback bloke, wrestling crocodiles for fun. Or maybe even a championship-winning Australian Rules football player, plucking balls out of the sky with ease. In case you don't know, I'm Irish but had events over two hundred years ago turned out differently, I might well be living one of those lives.

My distant forefathers were arrested by the British authorities in Ireland around 1820 and placed on a ship ultimately bound for the penal colony of Australia. I never discovered what exactly they did to deserve such punishment but during that period, people were being banished to Australia for such trivial crimes as stealing apples. As the ship rounded the southern coast of Ireland, a storm struck, forcing them to seek shelter in Berehaven harbour. The Dwyer brothers sensed an opportunity and managed to swim ashore. There, they hid in a cave and watched until the ship departed without them. They ultimately settled in the area, married and their descendants are there ever since.

Had they not been able to swim or had the storm not struck, who knows where they would have ended up. Maybe in one of Australia's convict sites such as Van Diemen's Land or Botany Bay. Maybe their descendants would have spread across the country, shaking off the convict 'stain' to become upstanding citizens. Instead of growing up in Ireland, I might have grown up in Perth, the very city I had just arrived in. I might have gone on to enjoy one of those Australian lives I just indulged in, bringing pride to my family and to the land of my forebears. Or I might have been employed as a customs officer by the Australian Immigration Bureau at the airport.

At Perth International Airport, the customs officer in question beckoned me to approach with a disinterested wave of his hand. He sported a short black moustache and his white shirt strained against his considerable girth. Absentmindedly, he asked me some routine questions as he searched my bags. Suddenly, he stopped his rummaging and froze. A smile spread across his face as he slowly produced a bag of dried fruit, holding it aloft for everyone to see.

'Bringing fruit into Western Australia is prohibited by the customs of Western Australia and you are hereby forbidden from taking it any further,' he stated, loud enough for the whole line behind me to hear. Or something to that effect, I was too shocked to remember verbatim what he said. I had seen the signs warning people not to bring food or fruit into the country but had totally forgotten about my illicit snack until now.

'It's only a bag of dried fruit', I protested weakly, 'I'm hardly going to start planting the stuff.' He fixed me with a deadpan stare.

'Bringing ANY kind of fruit into Australia is strictly forbidden,' he barked.

My face reddened with embarrassment as people tut-tutted in the line behind me. I felt as if a semi-automatic weapon had been found in my luggage. He clearly enjoyed his moment of power and I considered scoffing the whole bag in front of him out of spite but thought better of it.

'Enjoy them,' I muttered bitterly under my breath as I zipped my bag up. He waddled over a large metal bin and added my fruit onto an already impressive pile. No one will convince me once the day is over, the customs officers don't congregate around that bin and help themselves to the contents. If any are reading this and care to disagree, please feel free to contact me.

The incident with the customs officer had darkened my mood but that would soon change. I exited the airport terminal to the glittering sunshine of my first day in Australia. A dry, brilliant heat hit me as I emerged from the building and I blinked at the blinding sunshine and incredibly blue sky. I breathed a sigh of relief. There is no better feeling than arriving in a new country, excitedly looking forward to the start of a travel adventure.

I got a bus to my hostel near the city centre. There, I met Ben, a young English backpacker who'd arrived in the city a week earlier. After introductions, I got down to business.

'Fancy going for a beer?' I inquired. Ben smiled.

'Why not,' he replied, 'I know just the place.'

We made the short walk to the Brass Monkey, housed in an old Victorian-style building.

'So, what's the local brew,' I inquired, rubbing my hands together as I seated myself before an array of gleaming taps.

'That would be Swan, mate,' the barman interrupted, pointing to the locally brewed Swan Beer, named after the river flowing through Perth. I nodded and he filled a glass with golden beer. I toasted Ben to his good health and made quick work of my first beer in Australia.

And so, for the next three days and nights, the Brass Monkey became party central. To my surprise, Australians don't drink Fosters, as Irish television adverts had led me to believe. I put any sightseeing plans on the back burner and celebrated being in a country where my life wasn't in danger. The previous three months in South Africa had been accompanied by a constant low-grade fear but, once I touched down in Australia, that fear evaporated, leaving me relieved and ready to celebrate just being alive. An ungodly amount of Swan beer passed my tonsils during that happy time.

Once I'd finished my introductory party, I knuckled down to plan the rest of my time in the country. I realized I knew very little about such a vast nation. Irish songs such as *Wild Colonial Boy*, *The Fields of Athenry* and *Black Velvet Band* are full of references to Australia as the final destination for many Irish rebels. The little knowledge I possessed had been gleaned from the unreliable sources of television and Hollywood. As a child growing up in Ireland, shows such as *Skippy the Bush Kangaroo* and *Home and Away* gave me a simple insight into life Down Under. They enjoyed seemingly constant sunshine, lived near perfects beaches, spoke in a funny accent and said 'mate' after every sentence. To me, it looked like a vision of heaven. I couldn't recall any Australians I knew personally and apart from Sydney, Melbourne and Ayers Rock (Sorry, Uluru), I knew nothing of this giant landmass, the only continent that is also a country. I had three months to discover if the Australia of my imagination matched the reality.

Walking around Perth, I noticed the people were predominately Asian. Immigrants from every country in Asia seemed to have made Perth their home. This was obviously a city people wanted to come to. This wasn't always the case, however. For years, the authorities sought to keep Australia as white as possible by barring immigration from other neighbouring countries while actively encouraging it from Europe. The White Australia policy was finally allowed to lapse before being fully removed in 1973.

My wanderings brought me to a small park where I took a break on a lovely wooden bench. Studying a map of Australia on my bulging Lonely Planet guidebook, it became evident how isolated Perth was from the rest of the country. To the north and east lay the vast wilderness of Western Australia. To the west, the vast Indian Ocean up to the coast of Africa. Perth is closer to Jakarta, Indonesia (1,865 miles), than to Sydney (2,045 miles), Brisbane (2,239 miles), or Canberra (1,930 miles). The closest city of a similar size is Adelaide, over a thousand miles away. Only Honolulu, over two thousand miles from San Francisco, is more isolated. Perth seemed to be a beachhead of civilization on the edge of a vast and empty void.

This isolation also meant the city developed on its own terms, not influenced by the distant seats of power in Sydney and Melbourne. In 1933, Western Australia voted two to one in favour of leaving the Australian Federation. However, as the British monarch is also the Australian head of state, the outcome had to be ratified by the British parliament, who simply ignored the referendum result. Australia should really thank the Brits for that one.

Despite its isolation, Perth was clearly a prosperous city. I continued my city tour across the Swan River, where the glass towers of downtown Perth sparkled in the bright sunshine. Most of Western Australia's major corporations are based in the city, mainly devoted to mining and its salient activities. It's hard to believe mining was almost unknown in Western Australia before the discovery of copper in 1960. Since then, a vast range of precious metals have been discovered, making it the richest ore producer on the planet. Over forty percent of Australia's total export value comes from Western Australia.

As I wandered back towards the hostel, I felt myself falling for Perth. The streets were clean, the people friendly, and they enjoyed pristine beaches only a short distance from the city centre. I liked Perth. I liked it a lot. And that sky. They'll have to invent another colour to describe the unadulterated blueness of an Australian sky.

On Sunday, I made the short train journey to Fremantle. Known as "Freo" to the locals, Fremantle is the place where Perth professionals go to relax. It used to be a separate town but has now been swallowed up by a sprawling Perth. The streets were lined with nice bars and restaurants with plenty of places to get an ice-cream. Artistic vibes and a laid-back atmosphere made it the perfect antidote to money-chasing Perth. I walked along the Victorian-era streets of the historic area, adorned with beautiful iron-lace railings, curved awnings and pillared verandas. Is it just me or have we, as a civilization, gone backwards in this respect? How could we build such beautifully enticing buildings a century ago but not now? I'm no architect but to me, most modern glass and steel office blocks are unattractive to put it kindly. Fremantle's old buildings were works of art, standing on handsome streets and with bustling markets housed within lavishly decorated halls. Those buildings were made to be both functional and beautiful. When I thought of the soulless glass towers of downtown Perth, I wondered where did we go wrong?

Built by some highly skilled convicts in the 1820s, Fremantle Gaol was modelled on Pentonville Prison in England. I joined a tour of the prison and followed the guide as he showed us the cells. I shuddered to imagine the horrible conditions convicts must have endured in those tiny spaces. The tour continued to the execution room, most of which was taken up by the gallows. People on the tour seemed reluctant to approach the death machine and the guide had to ask people to come closer so everybody could hear him.

'Forty-four people were executed on these gallows while the prison was in operation,' the guide told us. 'The condemned prisoner was frequently offered a brandy to calm them before being given the last rites. A hood was placed over their head before being brought to this room. The condemned prisoner's height and weight determined the length of the hangman's rope, ensuring the fall through the gallows floor broke the prisoner's neck,' he said. The guide took the detached noose and dangled it from his hand as he continued. 'On average, death took about a minute and a half after the fall. In one incident, the rope was too short, and the prisoner's neck didn't snap. It took fourteen minutes of slow strangulation for him to die.' Everyone grimaced, turning away from the spot where so many had met their end, dangling from the end of a rope. Someone asked if the rope was the original.

'No, the original hangman's rope had thirteen knots. That's how you knew it for a real one.'

The room also included a chair where the condemned prisoner sat if he were unable to stand. When the trap door of the gallows opened, the chair fell through the floor with him.

With the tour concluded, I took my time to read the various displays concerning the prisoners. One contained the following newspaper extract, dated 22 April 1876:

"On Monday last, a daring and well-arranged plan for the escape of a portion of the Fenian prisoners, confined at the Fremantle gaol establishment was successfully carried out and six prisoners succeeded in affecting their escape."

The notice also mentioned the prisoners had been brought to freedom in America on a ship called *The Catalpa*. The name hit me like a bolt of lightning. A few years previously, I lived in Boston where my uncle invited me to see a one-man show called *Catalpa*. The play described the fantastic escape of the Irish rebels from an Australian prison. Standing before the notice, I realised this was the prison they had escaped from. It's such an inspiring story, it deserves to be a Hollywood blockbuster.

Between 1865 and 1867, British authorities in Ireland crushed the independence movement led by a group of freedom fighters known as the Fenians. Sixty-two of them were transported for life to the penal colony of Western Australia. In 1874, two former Fenians, John Devoy and John Boyle O'Reilly, hatched a plan to rescue the remaining Irish prisoners in Western Australia. They had become prominent newspapermen in Boston and New York and used their connections to raise enough money to fund a rescue attempt.

A whaling ship called *The Catalpa* was purchased, a captain named George Anthony hired and the ship sailed from New Bedford on April 29, 1875. Another

Fenian named John Breslin had gone ahead pretending to be a businessman interested in purchasing local property. Breslin convinced local authorities to give him a tour of Fremantle prison where he secretly informed the Fenians of the imminent escape.

The Catalpa arrived in Western Australia after almost a year at sea. The six Fenian prisoners left their work details and were brought aboard the ship, convinced they were free at last. However, a British frigate intercepted the rescue ship and threatened to attack unless they were allowed to board her. Captain Smith raised the American flag and warned that any attempt to board the ship would be an act of war. *The Catalpa* sailed out of Australian waters and returned to a heroic welcome in New York on 19 August 1876.

I'd successfully acclimatised to Australia and it was time to start my epic journey up the west coast towards my ultimate destination of Darwin, four thousand miles away. With no trains running along that route, I had to choose between bus or car. There was no freedom in taking the bus and hiring a car on my own would be expensive and lonely. Most people I spoke to in the hostel advised me to watch the notice boards for drivers offering lifts north. I made a few calls before agreeing to meet one guy called Dominic who said he had space in his van.

The following morning, I met Dominic along with Claudia who was getting a lift as well. After a bit of deliberation, I decided to go with them and within an hour, we left Perth behind and began the mammoth journey up the west coast of Australia.

2

UP THE WEST

'Hey Claudia, take a look at this,' I shouted as I leaned my hips against a phallic-like rock. She shook her head in disapproval, muttering something in German. Four hours north of Perth, we had stopped at the Pinnicles Desert, part of Nambung National Park. The moonscape desert is studded with limestone pillars of various shapes and heights, some over ten feet tall. When the first Dutch explorers saw the Pinnacles from the sea in 1658, they were convinced it was the ruins of an ancient city and it's easy to see why. The rows of shattered stone columns seemed to belong to an archeological site in Greece or Italy rather than the Australian desert. In fact, they are the remnants of a limestone seabed eroded over centuries by seeping rainwater. Over time, the overlying sands were blown away to reveal the rock formations. Some are jagged like giant shards of broken glass, others smooth like old tombstones.

Indeed, the Aboriginal people believe the Pinnacles were formed when ghosts had nowhere to go and became fossilized.

This ancient forest of stone had been millions of years in the making with no interference from man. Had they been situated in Europe instead of the recently discovered interior of Western Australia, they would probably have been demolished and ground up centuries ago for building materials. It was a time capsule, a place where nature had been the only force at play the entire period of its existence. That's the beauty of Western Australia, nature has been left alone to do its thing.

On the drive up from Perth that day, I got to know my fellow travellers a bit more. As Dominic drove, I tried to impress the lovely Claudia with my rusty German but instead, had her in fits of giggles with my grammar-free version of her language.

'I bought this van in Perth,' said Dominic without turning his head. 'Good size and handy for sleeping in so saves me money.' The van did a steady eighty kilometres per hour, virtually walking pace for such a straight and traffic-free highway. Cars, trucks and vans overtook us with ease. Dominic grimaced each time we were overtaken.

'Ugg, so slow, why did you pick such a slow van?' Claudia quizzed. Dominic just shrugged his shoulders and ran his hand through his sun-bleached hair.

'They didn't tell me the engine wasn't great,' he

muttered. 'Can't get anything over this speed out of her.'

We left the Pinnicles behind and continued northwards, rejoining a landscape surrounded by rough scrub and a harsh desert. The thin sliver of hot asphalt we travelled on was the only man-made creation for miles around, an umbilical cord to civilization as we journeyed across the alien landscape.

Shortly afterwards, I saw kangaroos for the first time as they bounded energetically along the road. I felt giddy at my first sight of these Australian icons, with their dog-like faces and powerful hind legs. I wondered what the first Europeans made of them when confronted by these long-eared, bouncing rabbits with large tails and a pouch for their young.

'I was warned not to drive at night,' Dominic said as light drained from the sky and dusk closed in. 'Apparently, kangaroos come out to feed and if you hit one, you could do serious damage to your vehicle. You don't want that problem way out here.'

We were an hour from the town of Cervantes, but we agreed to stop for the night. Dominic scanned the roadside for a suitable place to camp and pulled over at a sandy clearing about thirty feet from the road. I found some wood nearby and helped light a fire to cook our supper of beans and toast. By then, the sun had faded yet the warmth of the day lingered. I sat on a log, relishing in my first meal under the Australian stars. Apart from the infrequent hiss of a passing vehicle, we were enveloped in the utter silence of the desert. I had a few beers to celebrate the end of our first day on the road.

Dominic had a tent and groundsheet which he offered to me while he slept in the van with Claudia. I had my own sleeping bag so once I managed to erect the small tent, I settled in and found it very comfortable. It was my first time camping on my travels. Ireland's wet climate doesn't lend itself to camping, at least not the stay-dry-if-possible type I preferred. I settled in and pulled out the book *Mr. Nice*, which I'd been reading since Perth. The book describes the incredible life story of Howard Marks, at one time the world's biggest drug dealer and top of the FBI's most wanted list. Despite that, he comes across as a very likeable guy.

At some stage in the night, I woke and needed to go for a pee. Leaving the sanctuary of my tent in the middle of the night was something I had been dreading for a while. For anyone familiar with stories of the Australian bush, they tend to be filled with tales of poisonous spiders, lethal snakes and dead backpackers. A completely irrational fear gripped me that, while answering the call of nature, a sharp-toothed creature would spring onto my exposed member while in mid-flow. Trust me, in Australia, anything is possible. Snakes, spiders, thorny devils, biting ants were all realistic threats as I slowly left the security of my tent. I then remembered dingoes. Hadn't one carried off a baby in a famous case in the

1970s? It would take more than one to drag me off into the bush I thought, reassuringly patting my growing beer-belly. I put on my trousers, boots (hiking boots to withstand snake or spider attacks) and tiptoed only as far as I dared. As I relieved myself, I lifted my gaze from my business and was left open-mouthed at the utter majesty of the night sky.

'Australia faces towards the centre of the galaxy, not outwards as the northern hemisphere does,' said a voice, startling me and causing pee to trickle down my leg and onto my boots. I turned to see Dominic sitting on the bonnet of the van, shirtless, staring up into the dazzling vastness.

'I can't seem to stop looking,' he said. 'At the stars, I mean,' he laughed as I zipped myself up.

'I know what you mean,' I replied and we both fell silent, wrapped in our own reverie as we gazed and delighted at the starry, starry sky. It felt as if the Earth has been thrust millions of miles closer to the stars. In the stillness of the desert and amid that utter silence and splendour, I felt I was looking into the face of God. Humbled by the vastness of the universe, I felt small and insignificant.

The next day, we briefly stopped in the town of Geraldton for supplies but there was little there to delay us. Claudia begged to stay somewhere with a shower that night. I exchanged glances with Dominic, rolling my eyes at the soft German who could only take one night in the open. Secretly, I was delighted as I longed for a hot shower almost as much as she did.

'Might not be a bad idea,' Dominic said, as he scanned the sky through the windscreen. 'Wind's picking up, might have the makings of a storm.'

I rolled my eyes again, what the fuck did he know about the weather, I thought.

We ploughed onwards until we reached Northampton, where we decided to stay for the night. After consulting my guidebook, I found the address of a hostel and Dominic followed my directions as best he could. Darkness had fallen by the time we found the Old Convent Backpackers. It reminded me of the Bates Motel from the film *Psycho*, a tall, wooden building with darkened windows, surrounded by trees staggering in the wind. Streetlights cast eerie shadows across it, as if in forewarning.

It was cheap and, apart from three other backpackers, we were the only people staying there. I had a whole room to myself, a novelty for a traveller used to sharing dorm rooms. The spartan kitchen contained an old gas cooker and fridge that looked like they'd been installed in the 1950s. The lino flooring made our voices echo and sucked any warmth out of the room. Even the television was a large old set with only a few channels available. One of them had a show about the comedian Billy Connolly's tour around Ireland on his motorbike. It made me a little homesick to see those familiar landscapes again.

By the time I turned in, the wind outside had turned into the storm Dominic predicted. A large wooden crucifix above my bed banished any thoughts I had of self-entertainment. Once I switched off the light, I felt a strange and inexplicable uneasiness. The entire building seems to groan and ache with the billowing wind, like an old man getting up from his chair. Throughout the night, a branch from a nearby tree scratched at my window, keeping me awake. At least, that's what I discovered in the morning, having spent the night convinced some local lunatic was trying to break into my room and splay my guts across the bedclothes. I've rarely slept in a place with such a strange atmosphere and was relieved when we departed the following morning.

The novelty of driving through the Australian bush faded over the following days only to be replaced with sheer boredom. We chugged northwards past a never-changing landscape of low-lying bush with little to break the monotony. Even kangaroos had ceased to be a novelty and I hardly bothered to point them out anymore. What I did notice was the number of dead kangaroos littered on the sides of the road.

'Road trains,' commented Dominic, somehow reading my mind. Kings of the Australian roads, these trucks pull multiple trailers up to two hundred meters in length. 'Road trains are fixed with a steel grill on front called a "roo bar". They don't stop for anything, any kangaroo in the way is obliterated.'

'Broome looks great,' cooed Claudia, showing me pictures of the seaside town in her guidebook. After seeing the idyllic beach, I had to agree that it looked like the ideal place to take a break along the long route to Darwin. An hour later, I suggested making a detour to the Principality of Hutt River. Over forty years ago, Leonard Casley declared his twenty-nine square-mile farm a principality and named himself the prince. He declared independence from Australia, a claim naturally rejected by the Australian government and High Court. The principality has its own currency, stamps and passports.

'Sounds cool,' said Dominic in an unusual burst of enthusiasm. I nodded in agreement and looked back at Claudia for confirmation. This would have involved a detour of a few hours and Claudia wasn't about to let that happen.

'But do we have to?' pleaded Claudia. 'If we keep going, we can make it to Broome faster,' she argued, placing her hand on Dominic's shoulder. Feck it, I thought, she's good.

'Well, maybe we should just keep going,' he said, looking over at me with pleading eyes that said *do this for me and I'll keep you in beer forever*. I made a face and growled my bitter approval. Claudia thanked Dominic and sat back in her seat, basking in her victory. The principality would have to wait.

∽

After the disappointment of not seeing the micronation of Hutt River, I was determined to get my way at the next opportunity. I tried to convince my travel buddies why we should visit Hamelin Pool, which involved a dreaded detour. This time, no amount of hands-on-shoulders sweetness from Claudia would deter me. Dominic was initially receptive to the idea, but Claudia had no interest. At one stage, she had her hand on one of Dominic's shoulders, while mine rested on the other, each of us trying to justify our suggested routes. Following a combination of threats and cajoling, he reluctantly agreed to indulge me and visit the site. Claudia stormed off to the back of the van in a huff while I celebrated my victory by sinking a few cans of Victoria Bitter. *This place better be bloody worth it*, I thought.

After arriving at Hamelin Pool, we stretched our legs before wandering over to the shoreline. Protruding just above the shallow waters were hundreds of strange rocks, like solidified lava from some ancient volcano. I made my way along the boardwalk protruding over the water for closer inspection.

On the journey that morning, I read a piece in my guidebook about the significance of Hamelin Pool. The mounds were called stromatolites, structures created by an algae-like organism called cyanobacteria. Tiny particles of sand and crushed seashells are trapped by the sticky bacteria and slowly cemented together. Some of the stromatolite pillars in Hamelin Pool are nearly five feet high and took thousands of years to create. These tiny organisms existed 3.5 billion years ago when the Earth had no breathable air and no discernable life. The cyanobacteria turned light and food into oxygen. Slowly, they changed the atmosphere of the Earth and made life as we know it possible. Examples of this ancient bacteria are incredibly rare. Other stromatolite colonies have been discovered around the world but are inaccessible to visitors.

Dominic and Claudia joined me on the boardwalk as I squatted down to get a closer look.

'Is this it?' cried Claudia, scanning the horizon for some other feature she may have missed. 'A bunch of old rocks sticking out of the sea. Is this what we took a three-hour detour for?'

She muttered something in German before sauntering back towards the van. To be fair, it required considerable imagination to appreciate what these rocks were and their significance. It really is just a pool with some strange grey coral. If you passed it anywhere else, you wouldn't give it a moment's thought. It's difficult to comprehend that those tiny organisms pre-date plants, dinosaurs or mankind. They were the very beginning of life on Earth.

Dominic came over and joined me staring into the water. A tiny bubble rose up from one of the stromatolites and broke the surface.

'Wow,' I whispered to myself. I looked up at Dominic.

'Pretty cool,' he said before straightening up. 'Now can we get the fuck out of here?'

The van's lack of speed became a major issue as another hour spent crawling along the hot asphalt of Western Australia would be one too many. Shortly into the journey, I spotted a viewing point called Eagle Bluff and begged Dominic to stop, if only to break the monotony. Dominic obliged and we scampered up a gravelly path towards the lookout. I wondered what visual treat would be in store and readied my camera to capture the vista.

Once we reached the lookout, I stood with my hands on my hips and took in the view. It consisted of a sweep of ocean surrounded by cliffs. I scanned the area to see if I had missed something. Surely there was more? Alas, there wasn't, and I returned to the van feeling cheated. There had to be more interesting places to see than this sorry excuse for an attraction. However, the sheer mind-numbing monotony of the road made such pointless stops unavoidable. You simply had to take a break every hundred miles or so to avoid falling asleep at the wheel, even if there was nothing to stop for. I imagined some minion from the Western Australian tourist board scanning the map of the area, tongue protruding slightly from the corner of his mouth, before happening on the small bay.

'Eagle Bluff it is,' he'd say circling the name with red ink before rushing off to avail of happy hour at the local pub. And so, the Eagle Bluff award was born, the unwanted prize for an attraction barely deserving the name.

We stopped in Carnarvon to stock up on food. The town's main street is one hundred and twenty feet wide, designed to accommodate the camel trains that used to supply the area during the 1920s. Camels were imported from Asia to work the deserts of Western Australia. Many had been turned loose and now roamed wild. Beyond Carnarvon, we crossed the Tropic of Capricorn. This marked the end of the relatively temperate south and the beginning of the tropical north.

It was almost dusk as we approached Exmouth. We pulled over on the side of the road to gasp at the most glorious sunset – a good omen. After days of camping, I longed for a hot shower. I booked into the backpacker while the other two stayed in the van. Dominic was all smiles as he helped me carry my bags to the hostel. I could tell he hoped tonight would be the night with Claudia.

The following morning, I went out to the van and was surprised to see Claudia with her backpack. Dominic stood nearby looking sullen.

'I got an offer of a lift right to Broome,' Claudia said, barely concealing her glee. 'I met the driver at breakfast this morning and said I could go right away. He said we can be there in two days.'

I asked her when she was leaving.

'Any minute now,' Claudia said, looking down the road.

Five minutes later, a shiny and much faster looking van pulled up alongside us. Two English guys got out to help Claudia with her backpack as Dominic and myself looked on helplessly.

'Thanks for everything, might see you later,' she waved as they sped off. I looked over at Dominic.

'Tell me you got the leg over?' I asked. His face said it all.

'She said she wants to be friends,' he replied glumly, kicking a stone across the dust. I put my arm around his shoulder.

'Never mind, let's see what there is to do around here.'

Claudia had no idea what she missed.

When I saw the shark, I panicked. Sharks eat people, that's what I learned from the film *Jaws*. Seeing a shark while snorkelling was a shock but I reminded myself that no man-eaters inhabit Ningaloo Reef, and this was likely to have been a white-tipped reef shark, harmless to people. Sensing my presence, it quickly flexed its powerful fin and disappeared. That was only one of several incredible wildlife encounters I enjoyed at the aptly named Turquoise Bay.

Where is this wondrous Turquoise Bay I hear you

ask? Let me explain. After our sad parting with Claudia at Exmouth, Dominic and myself kicked back for a day. We shared a dorm with a deeply tanned Dutch backpacker named Ben. We asked him about any good spots to go snorkelling.

'You just have to visit Turquoise Bay,' he insisted, eyes widening. 'It's just so amazing, really, really incredible. Better than the Great Barrier Reef.'

That was quite a claim and I wasn't convinced.

'So, what makes it better than one of the biggest attractions in Australia?' I asked. Ben chuckled to himself.

'Hey man, I know what you mean. I wouldn't have thought anything could beat the Reef until I came to Turquoise Bay.' He leaned closer to us as if about to share a great secret. 'To see fish at the Great Barrier Reef, you have to join a tour and it takes hours just to get there. At Ningaloo, you just wade into the water a few feet from the shore and you're in a marine wonderland.'

His glowing endorsement made it an easy decision. The following morning, we rented masks, flippers and snorkels. After buying some food and water, we loaded the van and hit the road. A few miles outside Exmouth, we came upon the Holt Military Communications base, a sprawling network of radio transmitters and communications equipment serving both the American and Australian Naval fleets. Such an ugly compound looked so out of place on an otherwise unspoilt part of the country. Why would they decide to place a military base so close to a National Park? It's not like there wasn't enough room in the vast emptiness of Western Australia. That's military intelligence for you.

We soon entered Cape Range National Park where rugged hills emerged from an otherwise flat landscape. The scenery reminded me of a cowboy movie and I half-expected to see John Wayne riding out from behind a rock with Apache Indians hot on his tail. Sixty kilometres from Exmouth, Ningaloo Reef is part of Turquoise Bay and the world's largest fringing reef, stretching for almost three hundred kilometres along Australia's northwest coastline. It promised four hundred species of fish and over two hundred types of coral. After arriving, I could hardly believe what I saw. Miles of the most perfect white sand, lapped by inviting turquoise waters. Apart from a few other swimmers, we had the place to ourselves.

'Oh wow,' was all I could manage to express how I felt. I looked over at Dominic and he was already donning his snorkelling gear and heading for those stunning waters. I snapped out of my trance and followed his lead.

I entered an aquatic wonderland as soon as I entered the water. The snorkel allowed me to breathe while gazing into the life-filled waters. It was like swimming in an aquarium. Large shoals of blue fish floated by my mask, soon followed by a pod of bigger silver-scaled snappers. The coral was resplendent in bright orange, electric blue and blood red.

As I swam across a shallow clump of seaweed, my body brushed against something hard. That something turned out to be a green sea turtle. Startled, it shot out of the seaweed with very un-turtlelike speed. I was just as startled but once I realised what it was, I swam after it. Fully recovered from the fright, the turtle swam slowly and gracefully. I accompanied it for part of its journey, giddy with excitement. As we swam side by side, I briefly felt part of its marine world, thrilled to share the same habitat as this ancient creature. It was the first of four sea turtles I swam with that day.

Shortly after, I saw a small spotted octopus swimming nearby. I watched as it descended and attached itself to a rock, before instantly changing colour to match its surroundings. I couldn't believe how quickly it had camouflaged itself. I shouted to Dominic to come over, but its disguise was so good, I couldn't locate it to point it out to him.

After an hour, I decided to take a break and slumped onto the powder-fine sands of the beach. This set the tone for the day. Snorkelling in some of the clearest water I'd ever seen, watching the antics of countless fish, drying off on the sun-drenched beach before returning to the water. I felt the warmth of the sun on my face and smiled to myself. Days like that made me so thankful to have left my corporate desk job to travel. This was one of those special days, a treasured memory I'll tell my children about. This is living, I thought happily.

'Bit tired after swimming,' I admitted, slightly out of breath. Dominic cracked a slight smile.

'Why not use the current? That's what I did and there's no work involved,' he informed me, lying back on the soft sand. 'There's a good current running parallel to the beach. Just let it bring you along while you watch the fish.'

He turned his head to take a drink of water. 'Of course, be sure to swim for shore before you reach the end of the bay or you might be dragged out to sea,' he said, without the slightest hint of humour.

I did as he instructed and once I felt the pull of the current, I just floated along, barely using my arms or legs. It was fantastic. Since I hardly used any energy, I could snorkel for much longer. I caught my first sight of a reef shark soon afterwards. Not long after that, I spotted another one as it hovered below me in a deep channel of water, apparently waiting to attack any passing fish. It must have sensed my presence and disappeared into the dimness with a muscular flick of its tail. All I could think of after was where did it go and was it really a reef shark. I only got a short sight of it before it disappeared so I couldn't be sure. Could it have been a tiger shark, the kind that attacks people? Reef sharks are supposedly harmless but now, I wasn't so sure. Slowly, I became convinced whatever kind of shark it was, it was now stalking me, hiding out of sight before launching its attack. Slowly, I swam back to shore, trying not to slap the water too much in case I might be mistaken for a fat seal in distress. Every few feet, I looked back in terror, fearing the last thing I would ever see would be a set of razor-sharp teeth snapping shut on my arse. Whatever the statistics, I didn't want to be the world's first victim of the harmless reef shark. Once I could stand, I ran ashore, water splashing everywhere as Dominic watched with amusement.

'Everything alright?' he asked dryly.

'Fine, yea, no problems,' I lied as I scanned the water for a telltale dorsal fin.

Reef sharks aren't the only species that visit the area. At up to twenty tons, whale sharks are the biggest fish in the ocean and from March to July they feed in Ningaloo's krill-rich waters. Seeing one up close is apparently an experience never to be forgotten.

It was a day of pure awe and excitement. I felt like an astronaut floating over a distant planet, observing exotic life forms below me. I couldn't get enough. I swam with turtles, reef sharks, lunar-like pods of resplendent coral, blue-spotted fantail stingrays, squid, zebra-striped clownfish, silver snappers, and large schools of nameless fish. It was the same feeling I had when I dived in South Africa for the first time, that sense of awe at such a diverse and colourful world only feet below the waves.

As we drove back towards Exmouth into the red light of the setting sun, I knew I had enjoyed a day I would remember for years to come.

3

THE PILBARA

With no Claudia to consult, Dominic and myself were free to plot our next destination. We had two options; keep to the main route hugging the coast or take an inland loop rejoining the main road at Port Hedland. We agreed to do something different and strike inland towards the Pilbara.

The Pilbara is a barren region of Western Australia covering about 500,000 square kilometres and, with a population of about 70,000 people, is one of the most sparsely populated regions on Earth. This is mainly because it is also one of the hottest and driest places on the planet.

Driving through the Pilbara displayed the vastness and utter desolation of the region. Much like the previous day's travel, we spent hours upon endless hours driving on a road with little traffic, nothing to occupy the mind but low scrub for miles around, accompanied by the stench of rotting kangaroos killed by passing vehicles. The van trundled along at its normal speed of under eighty kilometres per hour. At times, Dominic drove with his feet on the steering wheel just to break the monotony. Infrequent passing cars provided the only other excitement as we both waved to the oncoming drivers enthusiastically.

We covered four hundred kilometres before deciding to stop and camp for the night. I marvelled at the brilliant sunset as I gathered wood, the glowing orb sinking into the red earth of the Pilbara. As we ate supper around the campfire, a blood-red moon rose on the horizon, taking the place of the departed sun. That night, I slept with the stars as my blanket and the moon as my lamp.

The next day, we stopped at the old mining town of Paraburdoo. As we strolled down the main street, I struck up a conversation with an old man sitting in the shade of a shopfront.

'When I first came here,' he said, 'the place was so backward, I broke my watch trying to turn the hands back two hundred years.' We visited a huge truck called the Jolly Green Giant, a colossal piece of engineering that carted millions of tonnes of ore during its years in service. Miners and massive machinery rule the Pilbara.

We drove on to Tom Price, priding itself as the

"Top Town in WA" due to its modest height of seven hundred and forty-seven meters above sea level. The town is named after an American engineer who explored the Hamersley range for iron ore and struck it rich. Mount Price holds the richest deposits of iron ore on the planet — about 130,000 tonnes of ore are mined each day.

Apart from pensioners and some retired miners ambling listlessly along the dusty streets, there were few people about the town. Despite how they looked, mining towns such as Paraburdoo and Tom Price formed the engine rooms of Western Australia, generating riches from the dusty earth of the Pilbara that fueled the national economy.

Major mining operations in the region had only started in the 1960s. Up to then, Australia was thought to be lacking in any significant mineral resources. So much so, the Australian government banned any exports of ore. That all changed thanks to a chance discovery. A miner named Lang Hancock was flying over the Pilbara region in November 1952 when he was forced to land during bad weather. After inspecting his surroundings, he realised the area was rich in almost pure iron ore. Over subsequent visits to the site, Hancock determined the iron seam he discovered to be over one hundred and twelve kilometres long and of an extremely high concentration. He also estimated it was large enough to satisfy world demand. Incredibly, a geologist named Harry Woodward had come to the same conclusion in 1890 but his report had been inexplicably ignored.

However, the find was useless unless the government lifted the ban on exporting ore. He stood to make a fortune, so Hancock lobbied the government hard to lift the ban. After years of being pestered by Hancock, the government finally relented. A mining boom quickly followed, and Hancock made millions from royalties.

At first glance, Karijini National Park looked like a solid candidate for the Eagle Bluff award. This is iron country and there's no getting away from it. Set in the heart of the Hamersley Range, Karijini only seemed to offer gum trees sprouting from shattered cliffs and spiky spinifex scattered across the rusty land. However, the real beauty of Karijini lay underground.

After a night at the local campsite, I woke early to get ready for some hiking. After emerging from my tent, Dominic looked at my attire and shook his head.

'I spoke to some hikers this morning and they gave me an idea of what to expect. Better wear something that can get wet,' he advised me. 'There might be some water involved.' This turned out to be the understatement of the trip.

Re-emerging soon after suitably clad in shorts and runners, I followed Dominic towards the Weano Gorge, the first of many that day. It started off as a nice ridge walk before descending into the gorge itself. After reaching the bottom, we walked along the floor as it narrowed. We came to a small pond, where the red walls of the gorge reflected on the still water, creating a perfect mirror image. I wondered how the hell we would get past it, but Dominic led the way, clinging to slabs of rock ringing the pool. He told me he was an avid rock climber back home in England and was clearly in his element as he easily negotiated the route. It looked very narrow with few footholds, but I followed him anyway. One slip would tip me into the water below. I didn't mind getting wet, but it wouldn't have been good for my camera. We finally reached a natural chute carved into the rock that dropped into Handrail Pool, named after the handrail miners installed for use on their days off.

Wandering along the bottom of such a narrow ravine, I felt I had delved into a cool and watery world beneath the scorched land of Australia. The cliffs were a mixture of deep red and brown, contrasting with the pale spinifex-dotted country surrounding them.

We left Weano Gorge and hiked the short distance towards Oxer Lookout. From there, I could see the junction of Weano, Red, Hancock and Joffre gorges. The gorges were very deep but quite narrow, so it looked as if the earth had been torn apart, leaving a deep scar behind.

'Fancy a bit of a challenge?' Dominic asked.

'Sure,' I said. 'What did you have in mind?'

We hiked a bit before arriving at Hancock Gorge, nearly one hundred meters deep. We descended to the gorge floor via a series of metal ladders. The air rapidly cooled as we descended towards the rocky floor. As we walked along, I noticed small metal plates fastened to the cliff walls declaring this to be a "Class Two" walk.

'Dominic,' I called. 'Do you know what a class two walk means?'

'Walks here are classified from class one to six,' he explained. 'Class one is like a walk in a car park. This is obviously a class two and so required a bit of care but still dead easy.'

He took a drink from his water bottle before looking at me.

'There's a really nice class five up ahead if you're game for it?' he inquired, raising his eyebrows in challenge. I hesitated before squaring my shoulders.

'Sure thing,' I answered hesitantly, 'But just what's involved in a class five walk?' Dominic smiled before turning to continue walking.

'You'll see,' he said.

The route quickly narrowed as before. Large pools blocked our way and the rock walls seemed too sheer for climbing so there was nothing for it but to swim.

'Jesus, it's bloody cold,' I squealed as I waded

waist-high into the freezing water. Hardly any sunshine reaches these deep gorges, giving the water no chance to warm up. The plates changed from class three to class four. We finally came to a very narrow section with a fast-flowing stream, walls of irregularly stacked slabs of red rock on either side. I fixed Dominic with a puzzled look.

'What now?' I asked. He pointed up to the nearby plate which declared this a class five and warned hikers only to proceed with caution.

'I'll lead the way and you follow,' Dominic declared. He stretched his arms to touch both walls and then jumped onto invisible footholds, splayed across the gorge in an X shape. In this fashion, he spidered his way along. I wasn't at all sure about this but had no choice. I copied his moves and, muttering a few decades of the rosary under my breath, made my way above the rushing waters. Dominic was fit and enjoyed this much more than I did, gleefully leaping from one side of the narrow gorge to the other. My muscles trembled with each move I made as I sated down into the rushing water below. Thankfully, I made it across without issue.

We finally reached Regan's Pool, a lovely pond surrounded by the most amazing circular rock patterns. We had the place to ourselves and so we relaxed on a slab and enjoyed the sensation of being in the middle of the earth. The surrounding rock walls are some of the oldest on the planet, formed over

2,500 million years ago when they were an ancient ocean floor that once covered the region.

It was tempting to continue our journey but the class six walk beyond required a permit to continue. We retraced our steps back to the top, back to the land of red dust. I felt as if I had just returned from a distant planet.

4

BROOME

I won't bore you with another description of more featureless terrain but suffice to say that the one hundred kilometres from Karijini to Port Hedland should be blotted from my memory. After an overnight stop in Port Hedland, Dominic was determined to make Broome that day and make it he did, reaching the town just before nightfall. After spending the last two weeks on the road, covering over one thousand five hundred miles, the plan was to relax for a few days in Broome. On our way there, I fantasied about the creature comforts of a soft bed, hot shower and cold beers. My heart sank when I discovered the Cable Beach Backpackers was fully booked. Instead, I resigned myself to another night in the van with Dominic.

We made the most of it by cooking up another pasta dinner, washed down with a bottle of wine. Afterwards, we sat on the beach with cans of beer.

Gentle waves lapped the shore as the moon's reflection shimmered across the water. It was a fantastic sight but not quite the natural wonder known as the Staircase to the Moon. This happens when the full moon rises over the horizon on a spring tide, its reflection creates a rippled path of light that looks just like a golden staircase right to the moon. It was a great feeling, getting a bit pissed in such a beautiful setting.

I checked into Cable Beach Backpackers early the next morning before any other travellers could gazump me. Let's face it, I hadn't exactly been traipsing across the Sahara Desert, but I enjoyed the hot shower to an unhealthy degree. I gazed lovingly at the cleanish sheets of my bunk and looked forward to a happy sleep that night.

Once my accommodation had been sorted, I got down to some serious relaxing. Broome is blessed with a laid-back atmosphere and the stunning Cable Beach – twenty-two kilometres of powdery white sand fringed by swaying palm trees on the shores of the Indian Ocean. In Broome, pretty much everything revolves around the magnificent beach, I've yet to see a better one and I've seen a few. People lounged around the hostel in hammocks, some cradling tall drinks and it wasn't even lunchtime. But why not? This was a place where time moved at a gentler pace. People seemed to be either coming or going to the beach and the only attire on view was shorts, sandals and t-shirts.

Anything more formal would seem utterly out of place.

And so, the following days melted into the sweetness of doing nothing, or *Dolce far Niente* as they say in Italy. It's a fantastic phrase and a great concept. My days soon took a familiar routine. I would wake and take a nice shower, slowly recovering from the night before. After, I would enjoy a leisurely breakfast with Dominic or whoever else was around, while enjoying in the warmth of the morning sun. Next, I might go for a swim in the pool before availing of the free bus to town. Afterwards, I'd hit the beach. A short run on the lovely damp sand to get a sweat going and then cool off in the warm waters. After, I'd lay on the beach and watch the stunning sunset announce the end of another perfect day in Paradise. That evening, I'd meet up with Dominic and a few other backpackers for a supper washed down with nice wine and beer. The party would continue afterwards on the beach.

This dreamy lassitude is known as *Broome Time*, where days and even weeks can easily drift by without notice. I experienced the same effect in South Africa in the town of Port St. Johns. There, it was called *Pondo Fever*, but it was the same affliction, striking me down with a heavy bout of relaxation for a week.

On one of those lazy evenings, I arranged to meet Dominic on the beach for a post-supper drink. When I finally found him, he was talking and laughing with a woman. I decided to leave them be and walk on but I was spotted.

'Hey John,' Dominic called, 'Over here.'

I smiled and joined them. He introduced me to Liz, a British backpacker working her way around Australia. We had a great evening recalling our travel stories while getting drunk on wine.

A fter a few days of this, I had enough relaxing done. I don't know about you but there's only so much of nothing I can do. I had read about a museum in town and decided to have a look. There, I discovered the story of Broome.

Broome owes its existence to pearl and, in particular, mother-of-pearl. The surrounding waters are home to the *Pinctada Maxima* – the world's largest pearl oyster. Broome once provided eighty percent of the world's mother-of-pearl, making it one of the richest towns in Australia. From as far afield as New York and London, buttons, knife handles, hairbrushes, and cigarette cases were plated with Broome-sourced mother-of-pearl. However, the demand declined after the 1930s with the invention of synthetic pearl.

Oysters had to be pried from the seabed by divers and in the early days, Aboriginals were kidnapped and forced to retrieve them. This practice of enslaving local Aboriginals was known as *blackbirding*. Pregnant Aboriginal women were believed to make the best divers, as it was thought they had greater lung capacity.

As the industry developed, Asians and especially Japanese were imported to work. Wooden boats known as luggers brought the divers back and forth. By 1900, Broome's docks were thronged with Malays, Chinese, Indonesians and Japanese. The legacy of that immigration is why the town centre is called Chinatown. Broome's Japanese cemetery contains over nine hundred graves, many deaths due to decompression sickness after being brought to the surface too quickly. Despite its isolation, Broome didn't escape the ravages of war. On March 3, 1942, Japanese planes attacked Broome, killing eighty-eight people, mainly Dutch evacuees from Java.

When I returned to the hostel, I spotted a poster advertising the film *Rabbit Proof Fence* at the nearby cinema and decided to check it out. Sun Pictures claims to be the world's oldest operating picture garden, remaining unchanged since the early part of the 1900s.

After buying my ticket, I took a seat in the colonial-era theatre. The place began to fill up as showtime neared. A middle-aged man sat next to me and I said hello to him. He was deeply tanned and balding, his face covered in white stubble. He reeked of booze.

'In the old days, the abos had to stand at the back

of the cinema,' he whispered, looking around conspiratorially to check if anyone was listening. 'Now they're showing bloody films about them. Some change, eh?' He looked for some acknowledgement, but I just tried to ignore him.

'The Japs and Chinks had it better, they could sit but only behind the whites.' He chuckled at this and glanced around as if expecting to see a row of oriental faces behind him. 'Only Japs here now are bloody tourists.'

Throughout the film, he kept making comments about the Aboriginal characters on the screen. I don't know why he even bothered to pay to watch the film at all.

After returning from the cinema, Dominic found me.

'I sold the van,' he said, getting the news out without delay. 'A Dutch hippie bought it from me.'

So, there it was. Our excruciatingly slow but dependable transport had passed on to another lucky owner. I hoped it would bring him as much fun as it had us.

'So, what's the plan now?' I asked hesitantly.

'Well, Liz offered me a lift to Darwin. She said she's in no rush and might stop to find work along the way.' He smiled and scratched the back of his head. 'Suits me just fine.'

It was the natural way of things as a solo backpacker. You meet someone like Dominic, share transport, stories, beer and then it comes time to part ways.

The next day, I said my goodbyes to Dominic and Liz as they left for Darwin. Dominic had been great company and a safe if overly cautious driver on the road from Perth. I'd miss his quiet but quirky ways.

I woke the following morning feeling glum for no reason. I guessed it was the effects of all the booze I consumed over the previous week. Broome was a beautiful spot, and anyone would kill to be there, which made me feel even worse. I also realised I was homesick. It was the annual Regatta in my hometown in Ireland, the biggest gathering of the year. I'd spoken to my parents and siblings on the phone, but they felt far away. Why was I here at all, I asked myself? What did these foreign lands have that I couldn't enjoy back in Ireland? The freedom of solo travel was great, but it could be tough as well. I also realised I missed the routine Dominic and myself had created, I missed his company and just being able to share a beer with him. I was on my own once more and this time, I didn't like it. I didn't feel happy and I longed to return to familiar friends and family.

After lunch, I walked to Gantheaume Point to see the famous dinosaur footprints. The actual footprints are 130 million years old. Unfortunately, they are about twenty-five yards offshore and only visible at very low tide. Instead, a concrete cast of the footprints gives you an idea of what you can't see. In any case, I enjoyed another unmissable Australian sunset with a group of picnickers. It was a fantastic setting surrounded by the clear blue waters and white sands of Cable Beach. To my amazement, a pod of whales started to breach just offshore. Everyone cheered each time one of them soared out of the ocean and crashed back again with a gigantic splash. That's one of the reasons Australia is such a magnificent place. Whatever glumness I felt evaporated in the reverie of the whales and sunset.

I had to find a lift the rest of the way to Darwin, so I visited some local hostels to see if anyone wanted to share a ride. I spotted a notice on one message board from a German girl named Sabine offering a lift to Darwin. Her no-nonsense poster told me this was someone who wanted to be on the road soon. I called her and we arranged to meet at my hostel. Since it was potentially my last day in Broome, I spent it on the beach, dividing my time between swimming and sunbathing. When I met Sabine later that day, I hoped she might be a close cousin to Claudia Schiffer but alas, not to be. She was, however, ready to leave the following day and offered me a lift. I readily accepted and was thrilled to be on the road again.

5

THE KIMBERLEYS

'Have you heard of the Gibb River Road,' Sabine asked as we drove through the Kimberleys. I shook my head. 'This is a road through the remotest part of the Kimberleys, the real Australia that most people don't get to see.'

Her face beamed as she talked about this and I found myself getting excited about the proposed plan.

'Great, let's do it,' I agreed.

'Yes, but the road is supposed to be very bad, very rough,' she said. 'I want to find out more about it before making a decision.'

And so, as soon as we reached the small town of Derby, Sabine made a beeline for the local tourist office. A balding, bespectacled man greeted us from behind the information desk with a bright smile and asked if he could help with anything.

'I'd like to know if it's possible to drive the Gibb River Road,' Sabine inquired.

At the mention of the word, the man's smile faded. He removed his glasses and slowly rubbed the bridge of his nose.

'The Gibb is not something that should be attempted in anything less than a 4x4 Landcruiser. Do you have one of these?' he inquired, knowing full well the answer was no. 'You would also need food for five days and at least twenty litres of water.'

He replaced his glasses and stared at us.

'Don't be fools by risking your car and your lives. The Gibb is a very rough route through some of the toughest terrain in Australia and is littered with broken vehicles much better than yours. There's so much to see in the Kimberleys that doesn't involve risking the Gibb.'

Sabine nodded silently, accepting the logic of his argument. I tried to change the topic to cheer her up.

'What about Tunnel Creek, it's OK to drive there, right?' I asked. The clerk shook his head but more slowly this time.

'Not as bad as the Gibb but still not recommended. Most tourists don't heed my warnings anyway,' he said in a tired tone, 'Go at your own risk.'

We left the tourist office in a gloomy mood. Sabine especially wanted to see the Australia of her dreams but now, it seemed foolish to attempt the route.

'Let's sleep on it,' I suggested. We booked into a caravan site where I pitched my tent next to her car and had an early night.

• • •

I woke the following morning to Sabine banging on my tent.

'John, are you awake yet?' I peered out to see her standing there in a business-like pose with her hands on her hips.

'I have decided we should try driving to Tunnel Creek,' she declared. 'Is this fine with you?' she inquired.

I nodded in agreement and said I'd be ready in twenty minutes. Soon afterwards, we left Derby and headed into the unknown.

A few miles outside the town, we left the comfort of the sealed road and followed a signpost for Tunnel Creek. I braced myself for a bum-numbing ride, but it didn't turn out to be that bad. Sabine drove slowly which made it much easier.

At Tunnel Creek, we parked and followed the signage towards the entrance, a giant gap in the surrounding mountains. I had expected a slightly claustrophobic experience, but the tunnel was huge, nearly fifty feet high in places and seven hundred and fifty meters long. As we made our way through the tunnel, the light faded to darkness. Thankfully, Sabine had remembered to bring a torch. We soon came upon large pools of freezing water which we had to wade through. Stalactites and their ground-dwelling cousins, stalagmites, decorated the cave.

Sabine grabbed my arm as her torch beam lit up a pair of glowing eyes in the water.

'What is that?' she squirmed, squeezing my arm tightly. I was as scared as she was but didn't pretend.

'It's a croc love,' declared an unmistakabley Australian voice behind us. He shone his torch at the pair of red dots. 'Only a freshie, not a saltie so no worries,' he assured us.

A crocodile is a crocodile, I thought to myself but said nothing, enjoying the role of protector.

'So, it is not dangerous?' asked Sabine in a tone of disbelief.

'Naw, these little fellas are harmless,' he declared, splashing past it. 'Wouldn't step on its tail though, still might give you a nasty bite.'

Sabine unfurled herself from me and gave the red eyes the widest berth possible, keeping her torch on them the whole time.

Further on, shafts of sunlight penetrated the partially collapsed cave ceiling, illuminating a pond of water on the cave floor. We sloshed through more water and even found a small sandy beach. The Aussie bloke waited for us there.

'This place used to be the hideout for an Aboriginal bloke called Pidgeon, or Jandamarra as he's also known. Bit of an outlaw, he was killed in a shoot-out here.'

The story of Jandamarra is a fascinating one. He worked on white settler land and became friends with an Englishman named Richardson. When Richardson joined the police force in the 1890s, Jandamarra, a skilled horseman and marksman, was employed as his native tracker. The pair gained a reputation as the most effective police team at that time.

Aboriginal people fought back against white intrusion by killing the settler's livestock. Richardson and Jandamarra were ordered to track down the offenders. In late 1894, the pair succeeded in capturing a group which included most of the elders of Jandamarra's own tribe. The group were brought back to the police station. During the night of October 31, 1894, the tribal prisoners challenged Jandamarra to choose where his loyalties lay: with the white invaders or his own people. Jandamarra made his decision, shot Richardson, armed the Aboriginals and began a guerilla campaign against the European settlers.

For three years, Jandamarra led a guerrilla war against the white authorities. His hit and run tactics and his vanishing tricks became the stuff of legends. Many times, the police had him surrounded only for him to vanish. It was only years later that a hidden section was discovered within Tunnel Creek, allowing access from the top of the range. Jandamarra was held in awe by other Aboriginal people who believed he was immortal. They also thought that only an Aboriginal person with similar mystical powers could kill him. He was finally tracked down and killed in Tunnel Creek on April 1, 1897, when the police recruited another Aboriginal tracker, Mingo Mick, who had equally legendary powers.

Mike, our new Aussie friend, joined us as we made our way through the tunnel.

'What's that?' I whispered. The faint squeaking sound became louder as we made our way deeper into the tunnel.

'Oh, just a colony of bats mate,' Mike informed us. He then shone his light on the cave ceiling, 'There they are.'

His torch illuminated a cluster of bats, hanging upside down.

I hate bats and I'll bet I'm not alone. They never did me any harm and I never had any issues with them. Maybe they just suffer from bad press as they're always depicted flying around Dracula or some blood-sucking vampire in the movies. My mother told me one got stuck in her hair when she was young. There's also a variety called Vampire Bats that suck blood from animals. Besides, they're basically just flying mice, reason enough for me to avoid them. Once we neared the colony, I tried to remain calm and focus on the ground ahead. My heart thumped like crazy as I sensed hundreds of tiny eyes staring hungrily at my bare skin. Suddenly, I felt something touch the back of my neck and I freaked out, waving wildly at my head and nearly stumbling into the water. My torch illuminated a laughing Sabine, hand over her mouth.

'Oh John, I'm really sorry,' she said. 'I saw how tense you looked and touched the back of your neck. Are you afraid of bats?' I said nothing and stomped off in a huff, water splashing crazily about my feet as I headed to the end of the tunnel.

After a short lunch, we left Tunnel Creek and continued along the dirt track. This was the real Outback as bulging boab trees lined the route and dust billowed in our wake. Windjana Gorge consisted of a lovely sandy beach meeting a glorious pool of water, banked by high cliffs on both sides. It was an idyllic piece of Kimberly heaven. The shade of the gorge made it a cool oasis compared to the scorching sun we'd spend the last hour driving under. The cool water invited – no insisted – a swim so I started to get undressed. I was about to dive in when I spotted a piece of wood floating on the surface. I then noticed it had eyes – a fresh-water crocodile. I scanned the water and counted ten more pairs of eyes before I sadly replaced my clothing. Swimming with crocodiles, even the "harmless" fresh-water variety, was not something I was about to take up.

Apart from admiring the unswimmable water, there didn't seem to be much else to do. I then noticed some people taking photos of something on the cliff walls. I wandered over to see what they were looking at. There, embedded high up on the limestone rock was the fossil of a fish that died over 350 million years ago. During that time, known as the Devonian period, the surrounding area was part of an ancient seabed. As I scanned the cliff face, I spotted fossils of other creatures. It was another reminder of how ancient this place was.

'John, are you ready to go?' Sabine asked. 'We need to get on the road before dark. I don't fancy getting stuck here overnight.'

Darkness fell much quicker than we had anticipated as we negotiated the bumpy road. We bumped along the rutted track, headlights swaying madly ahead of us. Suddenly, Sabine braked hard as we came to a flooded section of road.

'Oh fuck,' I said as Sabine said the same thing in German. We stared ahead at the twenty-foot stretch of water. 'I wonder how deep it is?' I said. Sabine looked at me.

'Would you mind checking,' she pleaded.

I hesitated at first, the water was flanked by tall reeds and I had no idea what variety of snake, crocodile or spider lurked there.

'OK,' I squeaked as I climbed from the safety of the car. I took off my sandals and glanced back at Sabine before slowly wading into the murky water. This is pure madness, I thought to myself. Wading into dark water in the Australian Outback at night was in the same category as filling your petrol tank with a lighted cigarette dangling from your lips. After quickly finding out it went up to my knees, I splashed a hasty retreat to the car and Sabine drove safely across. We were relieved when we finally hit sealed road again and made our way back to the caravan park in Derby.

The following day, we drove three hundred kilometres to Halls Creek, a small town in the heart of the Kimberleys. As we drove, the only radio stations I could find played country and western music from Johnny Cash and Dolly Parton. As we neared Halls Creek, we watched stockmen roundup huge herds of cattle amid clouds of dust. It was easy to imagine we were driving through the American Wild West and not north-western Australia.

As we entered Hall's Creek, I noticed the people walking along the main street were predominantly Aboriginal. After booking into a local campsite, Sabine wanted a quiet night, but I convinced her to visit the local bar across the road. As we approached the entrance, I noticed a police wagon parked outside, as if waiting to be called into service. A raucous noise bellowed from within the bar as we got closer. Sabine hesitated but it was too late to turn back. Inside, the bar was heaving with Aboriginals and everyone was uproariously drunk. I felt rows of eyes looking at us and even considered turning to leave. However, after a beer and talking to a few people, I relaxed. A few more beers and we both hit the dance floor, bopping with the locals. I met a girl who claimed to be the niece of the woman featured in the film *Rabbit Proof Fence*. That was the film I saw in Broome about an Aboriginal girl who finds her way back to her family after being taken from her home. Despite the amount of drunkenness, we had no problems from anyone. After we had danced our fill, we headed back to the campsite in very high spirits. This wasn't all down to the alcohol. I was thrilled to have finally met native

Australians for the first time in my travels through their country. It was my first time being with them in a social setting, talking and getting to know them. I found them to be a happy and kind people.

We drove the fourteen kilometres to Old Halls Creek the following morning, the original settlement founded after gold was discovered nearby in 1885. The ruins of Old Halls Creek looked like it had been abandoned a thousand years ago instead of 1954. Nothing remained but a few heaps of stones and the old mud-brick post office which is now housed inside a shed to protect the remaining walls. While tourists in Europe wander around the near-intact ruins of ancient Roman and Greek cities, almost nothing remains of the seventy year old settement.

Outside the old post office, I read an interesting notice: "Postmaster Fred Tuckett conducted two surgical operations here in 1917 guided by instructions telegraphed from Perth. His patient was Jim Darcy, a young stockman who had suffered internal injuries in a riding accident." This little snippet intrigued me and led me to one of the most incredible stories of long-distance surgery ever recorded.

When Jim Darcy's horse threw him on July 29, 1917, he suffered internal injuries that required immediate medical assistance. Darcy endured the excruciating twelve-hour journey to the nearest town, Hall's Creek. Unfortunately, the town had no doctor and could only offer the local postmaster Fred

Tuckett, who had a certificate in first aid. Tuckett was known locally as WBL for the "whole bloody lot" because apart from being a first aider and postmaster, he was also the telegraph operator, magistrate, commissioner for roads, protector of Aborigines and lastly the births, deaths and marriages registrar. Tuckett tapped out a message via morse code to his first-aid instructor in Perth, Dr. John Holland. Dr. Holland quickly diagnosed a bladder injury that required surgery, finishing his message grimly with, "If you don't operate, he'll die."

Despite being hesitant to perform such an operation, Tuckett realised that Darcy would certainly die if he did nothing. Using a pocketknife and without anaesthetic, he carried out two operations on Darcy lasting seven hours, all the while having to break away to tap a message or wait for a reply from Dr Holland. Tuckett was happy to report that after the operations Darcy had 'bucked up wonderfully'.

Dr. Holland realised the patient needed further medical assistance to ensure his survival and made the arduous journey from Perth to Halls Creek, taking a cattle boat to Derby before struggling the rest of the way with a borrowed Model T Ford. It took him two weeks to reach Halls Creek only to discover that Jim Darcy had died the previous day from malaria, a disease he contracted before his fall.

For days, Australian newspaper readers were gripped by the story of Darcy's struggle for life, none more so than Reverend John Flynn. Inspired by the story of Jim Darcy, he wanted to find a way to quickly bring medical assistance to even the remotest of Outback residents. He helped create the Aerial Medical Service, which eventually became the Royal Flying Doctor Service.

We left Halls Creek and continued the three hundred kilometres to Wyndham and Kununurra, only twenty miles from the border with Northern Territory. There, we found another campsite and had an early night after a busy day of driving. The following morning, Sabine said her goodbyes. She was headed for Darwin and didn't want to delay any longer in Western Australia. However, I had other ideas for my final few days in the great state.

At the campsite, I spotted a leaflet offering self-guided canoe tours of the Ord River. It promised a waterborne taste of the wild Kimberleys with camping each night. I was sold and booked a spot immediately.

At the ungodly hour of six the following morning, I was collected by Mike, owner of Ord River Tours. I didn't even have time for a coffee and was still half-asleep as I boarded the minivan. There, I introduced myself to Gabbi, a rather good-looking German backpacker and the only other passenger. I asked Mike if we were picking up many more people for the trip.

'No mate, just you two booked so you'll be on your own,' Mike said. I nodded and glanced over at Gabbi with a grin on face. That would be just fine with me.

If you're with me so far, you may have the impression the only backpackers roaming around Australia are Germans, English and a lone Irishman. For whatever reason, Germans certainly do seem to be the dominant force in Australian backpacking. There was little talk from Gabbi as we drove twenty kilometres outside Kununurra to the site of the Ord Dam.

'This dam created Lake Argyle, a body of water that has twenty-two times the capacity of Sydney Harbour,' Mike said with a proud grin. 'The water helps irrigation projects for the whole area. In fact, we've got enough water to last seven years, even if it never rained a drop in that time.'

We stopped at a spot below the dam and I helped Mike carry the two-person canoe to the water. I was slightly surprised as I thought we would have separate canoes. Mike gave us both an airtight plastic barrel to store our clothes, food and cameras. Once we donned our life vests, Mike went through some basic safety tips before concluding with a crash course on how to paddle.

'Are there any crocodiles in the river,' Gabbi asked.

'Sure, but only freshies love, nothing that'll harm you.'

Gabbi didn't seem too assured by this as we waved goodbye to Mike before setting off in search of adventure.

The force of the dam waters propelled us forward and made the initial paddling very easy. After a few kilometres, the river widened and the delightful dam current waned. Walls of red sandstone flanked us on both sides of the river. Sounds of abundant birdlife twittered from unseen crevices on the cliffs and from the tall reeds that fringed the riverbanks. As the relative cool of morning gave way to the rising heat of the day, I understood why it made sense to start as early as possible.

Gabbi said little as we sailed along the river. We tried to match each other's paddle strokes, but it wasn't easy. After a while, the river narrowed again and swept us past some submerged paperbark trees, requiring some frantic paddling to avoid a head-on collision. Once past that section, the river widened again to a lazy pace and we paddled hard to make any progress.

I spotted a sandy island and suggested we stop there for lunch. By rowing hard, we managed to beach the canoe on the sand and pull it safely ashore. I unpacked my lunch and sat on the soft sand, waving at passing canoeists. I felt I was on a real adventure and enjoying every minute of it. Gabbi stood up and brushed some crumbs off her clothes.

'I am going for a swim now,' she stated. 'Do you mind if I get naked?'

There were many times in the past where I wished women would have said those words to me and here I was, alone with a good-looking German girl on a remote part of Australia, and those much longed-for words had finally been uttered.

'No problem,' I squeaked, nearly choking on a piece of cheese.

She quickly undressed, her floral blouse, panties and bra falling to the sand in quick succession before wading into the water. Suddenly, a thought gripped me. What if this was some not-too-subtle way of inviting me to join her? I was never good at picking up these signals from women but as signals go, this must surely have been the mother of them all. Maybe she was into "free love" I thought eagerly, my mind now in overdrive. I fantasised that the next three days would consist of nothing but paddling and bonking. I tossed the remains of my cheese sandwich aside and quickly got naked myself, wading into the water to join her.

'Water feels lovely,' I said as I swam towards Gabbi. She seemed surprised to see me, smiling weakly before swimming back towards the shore, leaving me confused. I swam another good fifteen minutes longer than I wanted to, just so it didn't appear I had only got into the water to join her. Slightly chattering and embarrassed, I got dressed and we continued our journey. She didn't get naked anymore after that.

. . .

The river widened yet again and we had a lot of hard paddling to make any progress. At one point, the river narrowed again and brought us towards a clump of trees by the riverbank.

'Do you hear that?' Gabbi asked as she stopped paddling to listen. I stopped as well and strained my ears.

'Yeah, what's that?' I wondered, listening to the chattering sound. We paddled towards the source of the commotion and I smelled them before I saw them. The stink of urine surrounded a large colony of bats, hanging upside down from overhanging branches. As you know by now, I hate bats and didn't want to go any closer but Gabbi insisted, probably sensing my fear and getting me back for making her see me naked.

As we got closer, I realised the bats were flying foxes, a large species of fruit bat. When I say large, I mean they looked like bloody dogs hanging upside down in the branches, driving me demented with their high-pitched shrieking. This was the perfect nightmare for me, gigantic monster bats just waiting for some stupid canoeists to come too close. My heart raced and I couldn't take my eyes off the devilish creatures. God, I could see their terrible eyes looking right at me, sensing my panic. In a horror movie, the bloodthirsty bats would have chosen that moment to swoop down as one and latch onto my bare neck. I begged Gabbi to move away from them and I didn't relax until their wicked siren call disappeared.

By this stage, it was only an hour from darkness and we still hadn't found our camp for the night. We were provided with a map which showed the location of Colliman Camp, but it was easy to miss. We found it only after doubling back a few hundred yards, finally spotting it hidden in a secluded grove of trees. After tying up the canoe at the wooden jetty, we discovered a well-equipped camp with raised sleeping platforms, sheltered table and spring-fed water supply. After getting set up, we started a fire and made a basic dinner.

I produced a carton of wine I'd brought to celebrate the first night on the river.

'Fancy a drink Gabbi?' I asked with a big smile. She politely refused and allowed me to get drunk on the wine myself. She wasn't at all impressed by my behaviour and went to bed early in her tent, alone.

Foolishly, I decided to take the canoe out for a night paddle. Looking back, it was utter madness. If I had capsized, I would surely have drowned. None of that registered in my addled brain as I happily paddled away from the jetty into the stillness of the river, singing the Billy Joel song *"I May be Crazy"*.

The night was clear and bright stars crowded the sky. I paddled slowly, enjoying the silence and stillness. It was possible I was the only drunk for miles around. The reflection of the starry night on the water blended with the night sky so they were indistinguishable. After a while, even that faint divide disappeared as I glided through the celestial reflection, surrounded by twinkling stars. I laughed aloud as I guided my space canoe through the myriad of stars. It was an amazing feeling.

Bright sunlight along with a chorus of birds woke me at dawn the next morning. No chance of a lie in as Gabbi was anxious to get on the water early to avoid the heat of the day. Even though we had a much shorter distance to paddle, my hangover made it a tough day. Along the river, birds perched on tree stumps submerged in the water, drying their outstretched wings. Freshwater crocodiles floated nearby with only their eyes and snout visible above the surface.

We had lunch at another sandy beach before arriving at the second camp. A shoal of large catfish boiled the water near the jetty, obviously used to having canoeists throw them bits of food.

I took the canoe out again to do some fishing while Gabbi sorted out a few things at the camp. Barramundi is a prized fish in those waters and very tasty by all accounts. I heard of the fabled fish before the trip and fancied my chances of catching one. I had some fishing line, hooks and bait, hoping to impress Gabbi by catching dinner. She'd surely get naked again if I caught dinner for us. *Is that a Barramundi in your pants or are you just happy to see me?* I paddled up a nearby creek to fish and only managed to catch five catfish, which were as good as useless. I passed another guy in a canoe and asked if he had had any luck.

'Wait till you see,' he beamed before standing up and producing the biggest bloody fish I'd ever seen. No lie, it was nearly as long as his boat. Back at camp, I fried up the catfish and offered some to Gabbi, who didn't seem too interested. I couldn't blame her, there was very little flesh on them.

Next morning, we started on the long paddle back to Kununurra, slowly getting into a steady rhythm of paddling on the sluggish river waters. At this stage, Gabbi and I were getting on each other's nerves. While paddling in front of her, she complained about the amount of water I was splashing her with. When we changed ends, she did the same to me. The day was mercilessly hot with no shade on the open river. My hands were blistered from the constant paddling. I soaked a t-shirt before tying it around my head, making me look like a waterborne Bedouin. We both wanted to be finished with canoeing and get off the water.

Not far from Kununurra, we stopped at the Zebra Rock Gallery, where artwork made from the spectacularly multi-coloured rock can be viewed. I picked up a pair of striped bookends as souvenirs.

When we returned to the river, a group of elderly people had gathered around the jetty. They seemed surprised when we started to board the canoe.

'Where have you come from in that?' one lady

asked. Fixing my headdress, I stared upriver with the look of someone who'd been gone for weeks.

'Oh, I guess we've covered about twenty kilometres in the past three days, camped in some remote bush upriver.' This generated a chorus of gasps and led to a deluge of questions.

Did we have to bring our own food? Did we get wet? Were there any roads to the camp? I showed them the waterproof barrels and how we steered the canoe.

'Are you married?' asked one cheeky pensioner.

'No, definitely not,' answered Gabbi quickly.

'You don't have to be,' I said, winking at the crowd without Gabbi seeing me. They erupted into laughter.

'It's been lovely talking to you all,' I said finally, 'but we have to push on. God bless you all,' I said. I may even have given them a salute. They waved us off and were still standing there watching as we rounded a bend and disappeared from view.

I was very relieved to see our final port of call. Mike was there with his son and they pulled our canoes out of the water and onto the back of a jeep. Gabbi and I said our goodbyes with little fuss. At least I got to see her naked.

6

DARWIN

Arrival in Darwin marked the completion of the first part of my Australian odyssey. I felt elated at having reached this milestone and decided to relax for a few days and enjoy the charms of the Northern Territory capital. I searched for accommodation along the lively Mitchell Street and booked into a hostel with its own swimming pool. The poolside would be my home for the next few days.

The stifling heat of Darwin made sleeping a chore, only made a little easier after a few cool beers by the pool. Then again, what isn't improved by a few cold ones, especially when the air conditioning is bust and there's someone in the dorm with feet that smell like French cheese. At night, I slept only in my underwear and with a thin sheet draped across my lower body. Even that seemed foolishly excessive as the sweat rolled off me in little rivulets.

Darwin is the capital of the Northern Territory or

Top End as the locals refer to it. A territory? What is that I hear you ask. Australia is composed of eight states and two interior territories. Unlike states, votes from residents of the Northern Territory in federal elections are not actually counted. Similarly, elected representatives attend parliament but cannot vote and have no say in proceedings. This was obviously not ideal and so in 1988, the residents of the Northern Territory voted on becoming a state. However, they surprised everyone by rejecting the proposal and choose to remain a territory. Mind you, since the Northern Territory has only 1% of the population living in 20% of the country, they don't have any huge political clout anyway.

Darwin has had its share of misery over the years. The arrival of thousands of Australian and American troops during the Second World War turned the city into a military camp. It is the only part of Australia to suffer a prolonged attack from a warring force. Sixty-four air raids were launched against Darwin by the Japanese during the war, sinking many naval ships and severely damaging the harbour. A Japanese attack on Feb 19, 1942, killed three hundred people and destroyed many ships. It was by far the deadliest attack on Australian soil during the war.

However, it was nature that delivered the most devastating blow in Darwin's history. After Cyclone Tracy passed over the city on Christmas Eve, 1974, residents thought the worst was over. However, while Darwin's population slept, the back end of the cyclone hit. After midnight, the airport's anemometer was blown away just after it recorded a wind speed of two hundred and seventeen kilometres per hour. Sixty-six people died and over seventy percent of the city was destroyed.

The heat sapped any energy I had to go and explore Darwin and instead, I spent my days lounging by the pool. The locals referred to this period of stifling heat as the *"build up"*, only broken by the wet season in November.

One evening, I forced myself to leave the sanctuary of the poolside to explore Mitchell Street. It reminded me more of Asia than Australia. Coloured lights strung across trees and tables spilled onto the footpath as drinkers and diners enjoyed the balmy evening. Everyone sported shorts and t-shirts, women clad in light flowing dresses.

The very Asian feel of the city was no accident. Darwin is closer to Bali than Bondi, closer to Jakarta than Sydney. The city is also close enough to the equator that most days of the year have twelve hours of daylight, varying by only half an hour over an entire year. Darwin's tides are equally impressive, rising to almost twenty-seven feet in places during high tide.

Every Thursday and Sunday evening a famous night market is held at the scenic Mindil Beach. On Sunday evening, I joined a small gang from the hostel and headed for the market. We walked through the centre of Darwin until we came to the bustling market overlooking the delightfully named Fannie Bay. Set amongst exotic palm trees, stalls offered Indian clothing, Asian food, Aboriginal souvenirs and many other items. It was the smell of the food stalls that enthralled me – Indonesian, Chinese, Thai, Indian plus Australian dishes such as kangaroo and crocodile were all available.

With food and drinks, we decamped the short distance onto the beach and watched with hundreds of others as a spectacular sunset lit up the Timor Sea and signalled the end of another day at the Top End. Many of the people seemed to be locals and must have enjoyed this view hundreds of times before, yet the draw of such a natural wonder never diminished.

7

KAKADU

The sight of countless rows of salmon-coloured pillars was so unexpected, it halted our conversation in mid-flow. The jeep stopped and we piled out to investigate.

'Those are magnetic termite mounds,' said Darren, our Aboriginal guide. 'They can be over two meters high and their thin edges are always aligned north to south,' he said, leaning against a mound. 'The flat surface faces east and west. This design ensures only the smallest possible area is exposed to the sun. It's really a very ingenious temperature control system.'

I was hugely impressed by the earthen towers constructed by the industrious termites, resembling an eerie tropical cemetery. The mounds created by the magnetic termites are unique to Northern Australia and found nowhere else.

I had just arrived in Litchfield National Park, just an hour south of Darwin. I'd booked myself on a four-day tour of Litchfield and Kakadu National Parks with Gondwana Tours. Our group was made up of Darren, the guide; Carlos and Pete, a pair of fun-loving English lads; an English couple Ian and Rene; and Louise from Holland. Darren was an impressive figure with thick dreadlocks tied back under a wide-brimmed bush hat. Along with a pair of sunglasses he rarely removed, he looked every inch an Aboriginal Bob Marley.

Darren drove us to another astounding sight nearby where we found more termite mounds but much taller, some over twenty-five feet high.

'I'd hate to meet the bloody termite that made that', Pete joked. Darren didn't smile but explained they were made by the aptly named cathedral termites.

'The termites keep adding to the mounds every year, about one meter every ten years. The termites also have an underground tunnel system connecting each mound. During the wet season, this area can be saturated, but the termites are safe and dry at the top of their skyscrapers.'

Darren beckoned some of us closer and announced that the mound is actually edible, breaking off a small piece and scoffing it before our eyes. I glanced at Carlos, shrugged and broke off a bit before popping it into my mouth. It was gritty and tasted awful.

'Only kidding mate,' Darren said, tossing away the dusty material he had craftily palmed. 'I didn't really eat that shit.' I stopped chewing and spat it out.

'What the hell is it made of then,' asked Carlos, wiping his tongue with his sleeve.

'I just told you mate, shit,' said Darren, the faintest trace of a smile appearing on his lips. 'Termite shit, saliva and earth.'

As we spat on the ground, Darren turned towards the jeep.

'Come on you lot,' he said, 'time to head to Kakadu.'

K akadu is the largest territorial national park in Australia — bigger than Connecticut and Delaware combined. It is unusual in that it qualified as a UNESCO World Heritage site both for its natural wonders and its more than five thousand Aboriginal rock art sites. I spent most of the journey dozing in the back of the jeep. Just after we entered Kakadu, I was suddenly jolted awake as the jeep came to a shuddering halt. Darren peered into the forest foliage without saying a word. We watched as he got out and slowly approached some leaves, staring at them intently. For the life of me, I couldn't see anything, even though I stared hard at where he was looking. Suddenly, he lunged forward and caught something. He then beckoned for us to come and have a look.

'Frill-necked lizard,' he said, heading off the expected questions. It was essentially a miniature dinosaur, with long claws and a frilly cuff around its head that flared when threatened, which it certainly was then. The lizard hissed at us, baring it's small but sharp-looking teeth. After we took our photos, Darren released it back into the undergrowth.

Darren told us it was time to camp for the night as it was late, stopping at a clearing surrounded by naked trees. As we sat around the campfire enjoying cans of beer, Darren cooked up a selection of Australian meats – kangaroo, crocodile and buffalo. I certainly wasn't expecting such a good meal in such a wild place.

One of the obvious issues while in the bush is toilet needs. We had camped in the open with no access to running water or electricity. So, when nature called and the brown dog started barking at the back door, I was unsure what to do. I cautiously approached Darren as he finished his dinner and sheepishly asked him where to go to the toilet? He reached into a bag and handed me a spade.

'Shit shovel mate,' he said, enjoying the disbelief on my face. 'Head off into the bush and dig yourself a hole,' he said casually before returning to his food. I stared into the bush for a few seconds, wondering was this another of Darren's jokes. When no smile appeared on his face, I tentatively departed towards the unknown.

'Be sure not to step into anybody else's shit,' he yelled. Bastard!

I'm sure I was supposed to go as far as possible

from the camp, but I couldn't shake the image of being carried off by a croc while having a dump. Not the most memorable way to go. I selected a spot where I could still hear the chatter from our camp and started digging. Thankfully, the ground was soft enough to dig a good hole. I completed my business while constantly scanning the trees for danger. Any hungry man-eater who would have chanced upon me at that point would have scarcely believed their luck.

That night, we got ready to turn in and wondered where our tents were. Nobody had brought tents or sleeping bags as we assumed they would be provided by the tour company. Instead, Darren pulled out several khaki-coloured mattresses known as swags.

'You'll be sleeping on these tonight,' he grinned, enjoying the incredulous look on our faces. Again, I suspected that this was a joke and that the tents would be produced after he had his fun. Alas, it was soon obvious there would be no tents to protect us. We would be sleeping under the stars.

'Are there any snakes in the park?' I asked Darren, knowing full well there were.

'Sure are mate but not as many as before,' he said as he took a cold beer from the back of the truck. 'The cane toad was introduced to Queensland to combat the cane beetle, an insect that was causing great damage to the sugar plantations.' Darren paused to take a great gulp of beer, wiping his mouth afterwards with the back of his hand. 'Problem is the toad is poisonous to any creature that eats it. Once it reached Kakadu, huge numbers of carnivores disappeared. They reckon even the brown snake might be gone from here.'

Despite that slightly comforting information, we arranged ourselves in a grid formation with a mighty battle for the security of the middle spot. Nobody wanted a place on the outside defensive perimeter, where you were at the mercy of Kakadu's wildlife. The mattresses had a sheet on them so you could slip inside. Throughout the night, the sounds of animals scurrying through the bush kept me awake. My vivid imagination had me being dragged into the undergrowth by a crocodile. That's Australia for you.

Darren woke us at five the following morning, doing a very good impression of an army drill sergeant waking up cadets. As Carlos memorably said, 'It can't be morning, I just saw a shooting star.' That had everyone in stitches and lightened the mood of our sleep-deprived bodies.

After breakfast, Darren led us on a hike up the escarpment that surrounds Kakadu. He showed us a secret route to the top, which involved rock climbing, dangerous ledges and even an abseil. We finally emerged on a ledge overlooking the park. It was an amazing sight to see the vast forest canopy from our elevated perch. We felt like explorers who had just discovered a secret location for the very first time. In the distance, I traced the path of a small twister as it made its way across Kakadu.

After we got back from the hike, we celebrated by

going for a swim in Twin Falls, so-called as there's usually a pair of torrential waterfalls tumbling off the escarpment. Instead, we were treated to a weak trickle of water running down the blackened cliffs. However, there was a very inviting pool at the base flanked by dense vegetation.

'Is it safe to swim here Darren,' Pete asked hopefully? We all needed to cool off after the sweaty hike.

'No problem mate,' Darren said to our delight.

'No crocodiles then,' Pete joked as he headed off to get changed.

'Only harmless freshwater ones,' Darren said casually.

Carlos caused a stir among the ladies by wearing very tight trunks – the phrase banana hammocks was invented for his leave-nothing-to-the-imagination attire. We had barely entered the water when Carlos pointed towards the edge of the pool. There, a crocodile sat motionless, its soulless eyes peering at us. I'd seen freshies before on my trip and knew they were harmless but still there was a sliver of doubt. A crocodile is a crocodile after all. Nobody seemed sure enough to continue and Darren was nowhere to be seen.

While the freshwater crocodiles are no danger to people, the saltwater variety are a different matter. During the wet season, 'salties' make their way across the flooded plains to the base of waterfalls such as Twin Falls. Before the start of the tourist season, rangers must clear a ten-kilometre radius of any salt-water crocodiles — a huge responsibility. They're under massive pressure from tour operators to open the falls but no corners can be cut to ensure the safety of visitors.

A few weeks after our visit, tragedy struck in the very same place when a young German backpacker was killed by a saltwater crocodile. Their tour guide had told them it was safe to swim in the nearby Sandy Creek, even though crocodile warnings were clearly posted and it was night-time.

E arly the next morning, we made our way to Jim Jim Falls. After a good rain, the Jim Jim Creek thunders two hundred meters over the edge of the escarpment into the gorge below. However, like Twin Falls, only a stream trickled over the cliffs where waterfalls should have been. It required a lot of imagination to visualise how the falls appeared during the wet season.

Darren led us to the right of the falls where we followed him up a steep and sweaty trail leading to the top. Once we got there, we had to squeeze through a rock chimney to reach a beautiful swimming area. Along with the others, I relaxed in the lovely pool as water cascaded over my body. We returned to the base of the falls where we swam the seven hundred meters to a sandy island fringed with lush vegetation — pure paradise.

Back at our camp that evening, I sat on an earthen mound with a cold beer and watched the sun setting in a blood-red sky before a magnificent red moon also rose to take its place. The smell of Darren's cooking filled the warm evening air. It was one of those special moments that made me thankful I choose to travel.

Later that night, we watched an Aboriginal guide from a nearby tour group perform the emu dance, his body painted in white with his hands behind his back imitating the movements of the emu. As he pranced and leapt about the sandy riverbed, another guide played a haunting tune from the didgeridoo as the campfire sent sparks into the night sky.

'The didgeridoo is usually made from the trunks of dead woollybut trees, hollowed out by termites,' Darren told us. Those amazing termites again.

There was something primaeval about the dance and the music, something very ancient. As the haunting didgeridoo played, a sudden wind swirled around the riverbed, making me shield my eyes from the dust. It disappeared just as quickly, leaving me to exchange strange looks with Carlos. That night, I slept soundly in my swagbag. I was getting used to this wild outdoors living.

The magical Aboriginal dance was still fresh in my mind when we arrived at Ubirr the following morning. This network of caves is the equivalent of an Aboriginal art gallery, some paintings almost as old as the land itself. Kakadu boasts over five thousand rock art sites, the most famous of which are Nourlangie and Ubirr.

We came upon a notice about the local Aboriginal tribes, part of which had been obscured.

'Why would someone deface that sign?' asked Renee.

'It wasn't defaced, the local tribe did that,' explained Darren. 'The name on the bottom of the notice was an old tribal elder who died recently. In Aboriginal tradition, his name is not allowed to be spoken or even displayed. If people talk about him, he must be referred to without using his name. Everyone was sad when he died, even the trees cried when he passed.'

Kakadu is a culturally diverse region, home to Aboriginals from different clans with different laws and traditions, and speaking different languages, such as Kunwinjku, Gun-djeihmi and Jawoyn.

The main gallery at Ubirr featured the strange *x-ray art*, paintings of animals and fish as if exposed to an x-ray, their skeletons visible. There were also paintings of the *Mimi*, spirit-like figures that seemed to float and dance across the cave walls.

'These paintings are over twenty thousand years old,' whispered Darren in a low reverential voice. He also told us the paintings are often layered, meaning they were painted over again and again by several generations, some very recently. This represented an unbroken link from cave dwellers to modern times, unique in world culture. The Aboriginal people are surely one of the last surviving contacts with the ancient cave dwellers.

A small group gathered to look at the painting of a *thylacine*, better known as the Tasmanian Tiger. Scientists estimate the Tasmanian Tiger went extinct on the Australian mainland about three thousand years ago. The painting must have been made by an Aboriginal hunter-gatherer around that time, preserving the image of an animal now long gone from Kakadu. The last Tasmanian Tiger died in Hobart Zoo in 1936.

I was most taken by paintings known as *contact art*, Aboriginal impressions of the first encounters with white people. One image showed a white man, hands on his hips, while another showed the new arrivals most feared possession — a gun. The weapon was painted greatly out of proportion to the surrounding people, suggesting how feared it was by the Aboriginals. I was seeing the arrival of the white man through Aboriginal eyes.

Yet I was puzzled by the lack of any permanent structure built by the Aboriginal people during the thousands of years they inhabited Australia. I don't know of another culture that never built permanent structures, even the American Indians built stone dwellings high up in the cliffs. Maybe the Aboriginals felt they had no need for such things? Maybe they are more in harmony with nature than any other humans to have occupied the earth.

After leaving the galleries, I made the short scramble to the top of the rock plateau, which offered panoramic views over Arnhem Land and the floodplains of the Magela River. For the movie buffs among you, this is where Mick Dundee took Sue to show her "his territory" in the movie *Crocodile Dundee*.

Our final day was spent on the Mary River where we rented a small tin boat with an outboard engine. The river was infested with crocodiles, the banks strewn with large 'salties' laying in the sun. As evening drew in, I saw them slide one by one into the water as we passed by. Pete started acting the fool, making the small boat go sideways and almost tipping us over at one stage. If we ended up in the water, I wouldn't like to think how long we had before one of those crocs made their way to us. I was happy to get off that river, not a place for sightseeing.

We left Kakadu and headed back towards Darwin and civilization. Everyone chatted happily about hot showers, comfortable beds and ice-cold beers. I looked forward to that too but as we left Kakadu behind, I felt a little sad. For the briefest of time, I experienced something natural and pure and as old as the world itself. There was an energy there that came from the earth underneath my feet, the surrounding trees, rivers and rocks. They seemed to be alive in a way I couldn't properly understand. Kakadu wasn't just another park; it was the very essence of Australia in all its glory.

8

TO THE RED CENTRE

I n the late 1850s, exploration fever gripped Britain.
The nation awaited news of the expeditions of
Speke, Burton, and Baker as each competed to be the
first to discover the source of the Nile River in Africa.
Australia was also gripped by exploration fever as
teams attempted to find a route across the desolate
void of the continent. In 1860, the colony of Victoria
assembled a well-funded expedition led by Burke and
Wills. The rival South Australian government was
determined not to be outdone and offered a prize of
two thousand pounds to anyone who discovered a
route to the north where telegraph lines could be laid.
Both British colonies were cut off from the rest of the
telegraph-powered world and finding this route
would allow them to be connected to Britain. Glory
and a rich reward awaited the successful explorer.
Enter John McDouall Stuart.

By 1861, Stuart was already a veteran explorer. He

made five expeditions into the murderous interior, charting new territories and being the first to reach the centre of Australia. However, Stuart and his team suffered terribly on each expedition, many occasions coming within days of death. Stuart himself had been partially blinded from exposure to the searing sun. He also frequently suffered from crippling bouts of scurvy, attacks from hostile Aboriginal tribes and heat exhaustion that killed horses and even camels. In such unforgiving conditions, desperate people did desperate things. The explorer Ernest Giles became hopelessly lost during his explorations of the interior and only survived after finding a baby wallaby and devouring it 'bones, skin, fur and all'. Surviving such harrowing experiences was considered a great achievement. Far from being discouraged, once Stuart had recovered sufficiently after each harrowing journey, he started raising funds for another go. The allure of the Outback proved irresistible.

By the time Stuart set off on his sixth expedition in October 1861, the vaunted Burke and Wills enterprise had ended in disaster with only a single survivor of the merciless Outback. If such a well-prepared expedition could not succeed, how could a diminutive Scotsman expect any better? Yet by July 1862, Stuart had arrived at the sea near Darwin, having successfully crossed the continent. He never lost a man on any of his six expeditions.

I read about the little Scotsman as my bus sped southwards along the Stuart Highway, named in honour of the great explorer. Running 1,760 miles from Darwin to Port Augusta in the south, it roughly follows the route discovered by Stuart. The eight-hundred-mile section from Darwin to Alice Springs would be one of the longest bus journeys I ever made.

We made a brief stop at Daly Waters, three hundred and ninety miles south of Darwin and with a population of thirteen hardy souls. Many people scrambled from the bus to visit the famous pub, probably the only reason to stop there at all. I can't remember why I didn't join them, but I remained on the bus and snoozed. Before the pub became an attraction, Daly Waters was an important refuelling stop for the Australian airline, Qantas. I didn't know it, but Qantas stands for Queensland And Northern Territory Air Services – that tidbit might come in handy in a pub quiz some time.

After twenty-two uneventful hours, we finally arrived in Alice Springs. A shuttle bus from Alice Lodge Backpackers offered rooms and I was too tired to resist. I booked in with them and, after a gloriously refreshing shower, I felt human enough to take a stroll around town and examine my new surroundings.

As Alice Springs is almost at the geographical centre of Australia, I had expected a rough and dusty settlement. However, I was pleasantly surprised by a bustling city of twenty-five thousand people, a kind of Australian Las Vegas in the desert — without the gambling. It is safe to say that the town has prospered due to its proximity to the World Heritage site Uluru, formerly known as Ayers Rock. Almost every business in Alice Springs is connected with the Great Rock in some shape or form.

When I say close proximity, I mean of course in Australian terms. On a map, Alice Springs and Uluru seem to be side by side but this is another mirage. The Rock is over three hundred miles from the town. I had to remind myself yet again that journeys in Australia are measured in days, not hours.

As I walked around a corner, I almost collided with an Aboriginal man. He staggered in front of me and mumbled something incoherent, spittle dribbling from his lips onto his ragged shirt. He was out of his mind drunk. I walked around him and continued quickly, not looking back. He was the first of many drunken Aboriginals I saw that day. I felt sorry for them, a people robbed of their lands like the American Indians and the blacks in South Africa. Few people have a connection to the land like the Aboriginals do. It's not as simple as feeling at home or where they were born. They are in the very deepest meaning, a part of the country, just like a mountain is. Once their lands were taken, they lost any sense of who they were and became zombies, finding escape at the bottom of a bottle.

A few minutes later, I bumped into Carlos, Ian, Renee, and Louise. I was delighted to see some familiar faces again. In fact, it was bloody brilliant. When you travel solo, you yearn to share your journey with someone for a while. We joked about trying to avoid each other in such a small country. Renee suggested we go for lunch and in a short time, we were seated in an air-conditioned diner.

Over burgers and chips, I asked them if they had seen The Rock already.

'No, but planning on going tomorrow morning,' Louise said. 'Want a lift?'

Did I what? I agreed and it was settled. I was going to see Uluru with my travel friends the following morning. Things were looking up.

I asked them if they had seen anything interesting in the town.

'I visited the School of the Air this morning,' Renee said.

'Oh yea, I remember reading about them years ago,' I said. 'They have classes over the radio for kids on remote cattle stations, don't they?'

'That's right,' she said, 'The school serves an area twice the size of France. They used to transmit classes up to an hour a day via radio but now it's done through the internet and web-cams.'

'Must be hard to concentrate, knowing your teacher is hundreds of miles away,' Ian joked.

'Yea,' I said, 'plus you can get away with excuses like, "a dingo ate my homework".'

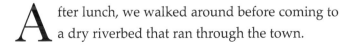

After lunch, we walked around before coming to a dry riverbed that ran through the town.

'They have a regatta here every year,' Carlos said, 'one of the biggest events in the town.'

'Oh, so the river floods each year?' I asked.

'Oh no, water hasn't flowed through here in years,' Carlos said. Seeing my quizzical face, he explained.

'Apparently, they cut the bottoms out of boats and stick their legs through, carrying the boats along. It's a proper regatta with every class of vessel you can imagine. They simply race each other on the dry riverbed.'

I laughed at the thought, I loved the idea of a water-free regatta.

'Best part is,' Carlos said, grinning, 'they had to cancel the regatta one year due to a flash flood in the river. Nobody had a single boat that could float.'

The following morning, I joined the gang in their lovely camper van and set off for Uluru. We drove a few hours before stopping for the night at Ayers Rock Resort. We left early the following morning to beat the crowds. I was giddy with excitement but also slightly apprehensive as we made our way to the site. I feared that my expectation was too high, that this world icon might disappoint in the way the Statue of Liberty had (much smaller than I imagined). I shouldn't have worried.

It's a truly heart-stopping sight when you first see it, an imposing mountain soaring one thousand feet from the sandy ocean surrounding it. Like an iceberg, more than two-thirds of its mass is hidden underground. Technically, Uluru is an *inselberg* or island mountain, an immense chunk of weatherproof rock over one hundred million years old that survived erosion when all surrounding rock had crumbled into the sands. This icon of Australia is located close to the geographical centre of the country. How weird is that? One of the symbols of the country is located as near as makes no difference to the centre of the continent. I don't know about you, but I find that remarkable.

Although named in 1873 in honour of Sir Henry Ayers, it is now known by its Aboriginal name 'Uluru'. Considered one of the great natural wonders of the world, 'The Rock' is also a sacred part of Aboriginal creation mythology or *Dreamtime*. The Dreamtime is the era in which Aboriginal ancestors created the Earth through their adventures and battles. Many of the paths these ancestors took merge at important points of the desert landscape, such as Uluru.

After lunch and a short rest, we returned to Uluru to walk the ten kilometres around its base. The red stone surface is not as smooth as it seems from afar, the sandstone takes on a more flakey appearance. The shape is also less regular, dotted with caves, gullies, and little valleys. Some of the caves contained ancient paintings, reminding me of just how sacred it was in Aboriginal culture. There were also spiritual sites along the way, many in the shape of animal parts, so sacred that we were not allowed to photograph them. There was a wallaby tail, an emu head and dog head rock and all have fables connected to them. Surprisingly enough for such an arid place, we also happened upon a couple of water holes. One is contained within a small red valley – the marks on the rock tell of the battle between two ancestral snakes, Kuniya (Python) and Liru (the Rainbow Serpent).

We discussed if we wanted to climb Uluru but decided against it. We read a notice in the Cultural Center asking people not to climb as it goes against Aboriginal spiritual beliefs. The local Anangu tribe calls the climbers *minga* which means ants. Several climbers had died trying to scale The Rock, mainly from heart attacks. There have also been a number of controversial climbers including a guy who hit a golf ball off the top and a woman who performed a striptease. More commonly, however, some climbers use The Rock as a public toilet, with evidence of their disrespect stinking up the sacred area. The climb is closed if winds are strong or if temperatures are expected to peak. These debates were rendered moot in October 2019 when climbing Uluru was banned outright.

After our walk, we joined hundreds of other tourists to watch the sun setting over Uluru. As the light faded, Uluru changed very noticeably from red to brown to grey. There was a party atmosphere as people drank champagne and watched the spectacle in awe. It was the perfect end to a really great day.

B ack at Ayers Resort, we sat around the fire with a few drinks.

'Must have been around here the dingo took that baby,' Renee said.

'What baby?' I asked. '*The* baby, the Lindy Chamberlain baby?'

'Yea, that one,' she said.

'Sorry, I'm not as old as you two, what are you talking about,' Carlos said, getting a playful dig in the ribs for his trouble.

'The Chamberlains were camping in this area in 1980 when the mother Lindy screamed 'a dingo took my baby.' The place was searched but no baby was found. The police started to suspect she had killed the child and pretended a dingo did it. It would have been the first time a dingo had killed a human, so the authorities were suspicious.' Renee took a drink before she continued.

'Anyway, with only circumstantial evidence, she got life in prison for murder. She had already served three years when baby clothing was found near a dingo lair and the case was reopened. Eventually, she was freed but it took another twenty years before she was fully exonerated and her baby's disappearance ruled as death by dingo attack.'

Carlos didn't seem interested in the story as he

practised playing the didgeridoo he purchased in Alice Springs. He had mastered the breathing and was able to draw a long deep tone from the instrument. Perhaps inspired by the day we had at Uluru, or maybe the beers, I decided to recreate the emu dance I'd seen performed by the Aboriginal guide at Kakadu. With Carlos playing the deep drone of the didgeridoo while tapping the instrument with a stick, I danced around the fire, imitating the movements of a slightly drunk emu. Out of nowhere, a gust of wind howled and swirled around the campfire. We stopped and looked at each other. There was something very unusual and spooky about that wind, which disappeared as soon as it had arrived. That was the last drunken emu dance I did. I do the penguin nowadays.

9

COOBER PEDY

If humanity ever starts a colony on the moon, it will look a lot like Coober Pedy. Situated about five hundred miles south of Alice Springs in the unforgiving Outback, the town is famous for two things — opal mining and people living in underground caves. I couldn't wait to see it.

The Underground Backpacker in Coober Pedy was just like any other hostel except the dorms are six meters underground. After checking in, I was handed a set of bed sheets and a towel. I expected a key for the dorm room and when none appeared, I asked for one.

'No key mate,' smiled the owner. 'You'll see when you get to your room.'

The air cooled noticeably as I descended into the bowels of the rock-hewn dwelling. When I found my room, I laughed. The 'dorms' were caves off a central passage with no doors and no need for any keys.

After settling in, I took a walk around the town. Coober Pedy owes its existence to opal, supplying much of the world's total demand. Prospectors flocked here after fourteen-year-old Willie Hutchison wandered off from his campsite in 1915 and found opals in fabulous amounts. It's still the biggest opal discovery in the world by a huge margin.

Mushroom-shaped vents sprouted from the low hills, betraying homes hewn from the rock. About one-third of residents live in underground caves called *dugouts*. It's cost-effective and the sandstone dwellings hold a constant temperature of twenty-three degrees Celsius. You have the added bonus of possibly finding opals while digging your home. There are plenty of stories of people extending their dugouts only to hit fabulous veins of opal, making them filthy rich. One example is the Experience Motel. The owner wanted to make an extension of six meters, but his wife insisted on seven. They discovered a fortune of opals in that extra meter. Things like that happen a lot around there.

I have my own theory on why the good folk of Coober Pedy decided to live underground. They claim it's due to the extreme heat but If that was the case, half of Northern Australia should be living in burrows under the earth. Instead, I think it's much more likely that the residents got together some years ago to help their ailing town. They needed a gimmick to attract tourists. A town with a population that lived in caves sounded great, so they voted to move underground and thus, the legend of Coober Pedy was born. Just my own theory but it does make you think.

Disused mining equipment, broken generators, and car wrecks lay scattered around the town. There didn't seem to be any effort to remove the debris. It gives the place a real working feel, a place where you'd half expect Mad Max to come roaring around a corner, driving some crazy vehicle fashioned from the junk that the town discards.

The following morning, I joined a tour of Coober Pedy. Our first stop was the graveyard. Our guide led us to the final resting place of one of the town's most interesting characters.

'This is the grave of Karl Bratz,' our guide informed us, pointing at the unusual burial site, unusual because the grave was marked by a steel beer barrel instead of a headstone.

'Karl, like most people in this town, was an opal miner,' continued the guide. 'Karl was also an alcoholic but a very lovable and well-liked guy. After he discovered he had a terminal illness, he took out a large bank loan. He used the proceeds to have himself one hell of a bender before he finally passed away.'

The guide smiled to himself at the coming joke.

'It was only after his death that his wife discovered the loan and the fact she was liable for the payments.'

After the laughter died down, the guide placed his hand on the barrel.

'One of his final wishes was to be buried in a corrugated-iron coffin and to have a full keg of beer as his headstone so that everyone could have a drink on him.'

Those very words were inscribed on his keg, proving this was a man who enjoyed life to the very end. I'm not sure if his poor wife would share the same sentiment.

On the way back to the bus, I caught up with a very attractive blonde woman I spotted earlier and attempted to charm her with my Irish wit.

'That's the way I want to be buried,' I said grinning, 'with a keg of beer as my headstone.' She turned her head towards me, but a pair of gigantic sunglasses hid most of her face.

'Where are you from?' I asked.

'Denmark,' she whispered before hurrying back to the minivan.

Once on board, she quickly inserted her earphones which ended any chance to continue the thrilling conversation. Nothing ventured, nothing gained I thought as I slid into my seat and imagined what she would look like naked.

A fter leaving the cemetery, we drove past an expanse of barren ground. The guide slowed the minivan and pointed out the window.

'This is Coober Pedy Golf Course,' he said, pointing to the grassless ground.

Normally, I would have assumed it was a joke, but anything is possible in this crazy town.

'As you can see, the course is not covered in grass so players must carry their own patch of artificial turf when they play.'

There were more howls of laughter and guffawing.

'The balls used are luminous yellow. This means that golf can be played late in the evening when light is poorer but heat and flies are more bearable. It also prevents emus from stealing the balls by mistaking white golf balls for their eggs.'

While this may seem to be one of the strangest golf courses in the world, I remembered there's an eight-hundred-and-fifty miles long course that spans the Nullarbor Plain of southern Australia. Now that's bonkers. As we pulled away, I saw a tongue-in-cheek sign warning players to "Keep off the Grass".

I had been looking forward to our next stop, the underground lair of Crocodile Harry. Harry lived in his own version of a subterranean playboy mansion, lavishly decorated with women's bras, knickers, nude calendars and statues of enormous-breasted beauties. Harry himself sat contentedly in his chair, observing the crowd as they wandered around his home. He chomped on a smokeless pipe while his arms rested on his lap, reminding me of an aged Popeye.

However, it seemed he had lived another life

before tourists found him. A large black-and-white photograph hung on his cave wall showing him alongside an eight-meter long crocodile he had killed. I couldn't tell if the beast in the photo was real, it just looked too large to be natural. It must have taken enormous effort and strength to trap and kill something as powerful as that. He had been a crocodile hunter before coming to Coober Pedy and was reputed to be the inspiration for the character Mick Dundee in *Crocodile Dundee*. From crocs to crotchless-undies, where had it all gone wrong?

'Would you mind taking a photo for me?' I turned around to see the Danish blonde I'd met earlier.

'Sure,' I grinned, taking the camera from her. She approached Harry and asked him for a photo. He flashed a big toothless smile and invited her onto his knee.

'OK,' I said, 'One, two, three, cheese.'

Just as I clicked the button, Harry darted his hands onto her breasts, smiling like a naughty boy. She seemed shocked for an instant but then laughed. It was Harry after all.

After departing Harry's cave, we drove out of town. There are over 250,000 mine shafts around Coober Pedy marked by distinctive piles of rubble, making the surrounding area look like it's been infested by giant moles. Signs warned visitors to walk carefully and keep their eyes open.

We stopped at a long wire fence in the middle of the desert and got out of the van.

'This is the famous Australian dog fence,' declared our guide, pointing to the wire barrier nearby. 'The fence is six feet high and over three thousand miles long, running from the coast of South Australia right up to eastern Queensland, making it twice as long as the Great Wall of China. The barrier is there for one purpose: to stop dingoes, the wild dogs of Australia, from killing sheep in the predominantly farming lands of south-east Australia.'

I could barely comprehend this, a wire mesh fence running across an entire continent. It's one thing to attempt this on normal terrain but across a deadly desert is another. I asked the guide who was responsible for looking after the barrier.

'The fence is maintained by a government department and employs about twenty-five people. Each two-hundred-kilometre section is maintained by a team of two, who must go out and check it every day, repairing any damage.'

Was the fence effective at keeping dingoes out, someone asked.

'Sheep farmers probably think so. Without it, the sheep industry would be decimated. Australia exports over four billion Australian dollars (five billion US dollars) every year. A lot of jobs and money depend on this fence.'

Our next stop was at the top of a valley, where we saw an endless expanse of barren desert. A few small hills protruded from the desert on this otherwise featureless wasteland.

'This is called the Breakaways,' our guide said, waving a hand towards the desert. 'Named after those hills you see that seem to have broken away from the main ridge. This is where they shot movies such as *Mad Max* and *Priscilla Queen of the Desert*.'

Thread-like cracks of long-gone streams decorated the rust-coloured landscape, giving it a very lunar feel. I half expected to see a space rover carrying some astronauts bouncing over the rocky terrain at any moment.

'All this was once part of a huge inland sea, millions of years ago,' our guide continued. 'If you walk along the ground out there, you're walking on an ancient seabed. There are even fossilized shells scattered about the place.'

After being dropped back to Coober Pedy that evening, I went for supper in a Greek restaurant not far from the hostel. The menu was surprisingly good, and I ordered a feta salad washed down with beer. Greek music played from the sound system and if I closed my eyes, I could almost imagine I was on holiday in Crete and not in the middle of the Australian Outback.

Once the meal was finished, I decided to go to mass. Now, I wouldn't be a regular mass-goer by any means but the Catholic church in Coober Pedy was special. You guessed it — the church of St Peter and Paul's was built underground, like a small Roman catacomb. It was also tiny with seating for about twenty-five worshippers.

I took a seat and waited for the mass to start. A regular churchgoer obviously noticed the new face and approached me.

'Would you do a reading for us?' she asked. This tends to happen to me a lot when I attend mass in foreign countries. I'm not sure why. Maybe I look especially devout, or maybe I'm in need of a place nearer to the altar, who knows.

Fifteen minutes late, the priest finally arrived, hurrying towards the altar with his heavy boots clattering on the stone floor. Offering his sincere apologies, he told us he had been hiking with friends and lost track of time.

After mass finished, the priest thanked me for doing the reading and introduced himself.

'I came here years ago and love the feeling of the place. It really draws you in.'

I asked him about his parish.

'It's a big one,' he said, 'do you happen to have a map?'

I produced my guidebook and showed him the map of Australia. He drew his finger across the boundaries of his parish. It went up to Uluru, touched Western Australia, Northern Territory, Queensland, and New South Wales. This priest was responsible for a parish bigger than Texas, surely a world record.

As I walked back to the hostel, I passed the Greek restaurant owner and he waved at me. I wasn't even there a day but already, I knew someone. I got the sense that everyone in town knew each other and watched out for one another. This was their place, their tribe, their people. There was a camaraderie only found in far-flung outposts such as this. The locals were also fiercely independent and wary of any outside interests that might want to overly commercialize opal mining. Many came to strike it rich and get the hell out. They ended up staying, somehow drawn to the place, living and working in their burrows, getting used to life underground and away from authority.

While most mining in Australia had long-since been taken over by big corporations, Coober Pedy kept the prospector spirit alive. Even when the chain store Woolworths tried to move in, they were threatened with being blown up.

It was my last evening in Coober Pedy and I wanted to have a go at noodling to see if I could strike it rich. Noodling, also known as fossicking, means sifting through the rubble in search of small gems missed by the miners. The gems are easy enough to spot, opals are the only ones with more than one colour, and their unearthly sparkle shows in the rough soil. Bright opals fetch more per carat than diamonds so this was a pastime that could potentially make me serious money.

As I searched the earth and stones, I indulged in a happy daydream of what it would be like to catch a glimpse of that famous flash of brilliance. I imagined it would be valued at thousands of dollars and I'd travel in style for the rest of my time in Australia, tipping waiters with thick wads of notes and buying rounds of beer at bars. I then understood why people stay. They stay for the opportunity that one day they'll hit a rich seam of gems and never have to work again. A very small sense of that gripped me as I scanned the debris for that glint that would change my life. I was surprised to find that I'd spent almost two hours there. I think some residents of Coober Pedy are surprised to find years have gone by, all the while searching for that elusive sparkle.

10

ADELAIDE

I've stayed in some strange places in my time, but Adelaide City Backpackers will take some beating. As I checked in, the lady behind the reception leaned across the counter until she was only inches from my face.

'Just to let you know, my husband's a retired police officer,' she said before handing me my sheets and showing me to my dorm room.

The place felt more like a stately home than a modern hostel, cluttered with knick-knacks collected over the years, including two female mannequins standing at the small bar. However, free continental breakfast plus apple pie and ice cream for supper made up for the weird surroundings. I soon discovered that Pam, the strange lady at reception, ran the hostel along with her ex-policeman husband.

What made the place so unusual was that there were warning signs everywhere, such as,

"This room is private. How would you like it if I went to your house and had a nosy, you wouldn't like it, would ya? [signed] The Owner."

Really gives you that welcoming feeling, doesn't it? There was an old chest in the living room that had a similar warning,

"Keep off this chest, it's over 100 years old. [signed] The Owner."

In the kitchen, another one read,

"We provide you with free tea and coffee, continental breakfast, apple pie, put up with pilfering and get really pissed off when you thank us by booking tours through other hostels. [signed] The Owner."

For me, the best one hung behind a large stuffed chair in the living room – it simply read,

"The Owner"

At breakfast the following morning, I met Pam as I helped myself to some cornflakes.

'Backpackers are so filthy and lazy, never want to clean up after themselves,' she told me while topping up the cereal containers.

Was she for real?

'Japan, come here and clean up this area,' she shouted at one of her staff.

I later learned that this poor girl was in fact from China, but that Pam refers to her as "Japan", never bothering to learn her name or true country of origin.

Copies of a police magazine were strategically placed around the common area, as a reminder to us backpacker vermin that we were being watched. I was idly browsing through one of those magazines when I heard a familiar voice.

'I don't bloody believe it...John?'

I looked up to see Carlos's beaming face. We shared a brief hug before Louise, Ian, and Renee joined us. They told me they rented a camper van and planned to leave the following morning for Melbourne.

'You know what I'm gonna say, mate,' Carlos said, resting his hand on my shoulder. 'It's bloody fate, why fight it?'

He was right of course. Whatever sightseeing plans I had for Adelaide would have to wait. The Gods had determined that I would spend my time with this lot. I was bloody delighted.

When I left the hostel the following morning, my stomach was doing cartwheels and I didn't feel well. Had Pam poisoned the apple pie and custard last night in an attempt to get rid of the backpacker filth that invaded her home? Jokes would have to wait as I deteriorated badly. I met up with the gang and boarded the lovely six-berth camper van, setting a course towards Melbourne. Carlos drove as I lay crumbled in the back, oblivious to any passing scenery. Even when we drove through the beautiful Grampians National Park, I never bothered to look out the window and couldn't care less about sightseeing. The others marvelled at the woods and mountains while I wished for a speedy death.

Sometime later, Ian woke me from my fitful sleep.

'John, we're on the Great Ocean Road,' he told me. The name of the famous road helped summon some reserves of strength and I sat up to look out the window. The Great Ocean Road hugs the southeastern coast of Victoria. It was built between 1919 and 1932 by soldiers to commemorate the dead of the First World War, making it the world's largest war memorial. Its construction also provided much-needed work during depression times. I watched the passing scenery as the road wound its way along the coast following dramatic limestone cliffs towering above the ocean. The coastal area is dotted with rock stacks, arches, grottos, and blowholes.

The gang got out to look at London Bridge, a rock arch standing alone offshore which was once connected to the mainland. Visitors would run across the precarious walkway to access the seaward section. All that activity can't have been good because the bridge section collapsed in 1990, sending tons of rock debris into the surf below and stranding two startled but miraculously unharmed tourists. The two were rescued by helicopter amid huge media coverage. Apparently, it turned out they were married but not to each other. What were the chances?

The fresh air made me feel better and I felt good enough to join the others when they stopped at the viewpoint for the Twelve Apostles, famous limestone sea stacks in a beautiful formation just off the coast. I couldn't believe how windy it was and once I took my photo, I returned to the camper as quickly as I could.

For the remainder of the journey, I lay in the back and felt the winding road swing me gently back and forth until I fell into a deep sleep. When I woke, we had arrived in Melbourne. I felt better and managed to have some soup that evening. I was relieved to be making a recovery as I had booked a flight the following morning to a place with significant connections to Ireland, a place of devils and dungeons.

I was off to Tasmania.

11

TASMANIA

My interest in Tasmania started long before I arrived on the island. Tasmania was discovered by the Dutch explorer Abel Tasman in 1642. He named his new discovery Van Diemen's Land after the governor of the Dutch East Indies, present-day Indonesia. Growing up in Ireland, Van Diemen's Land featured regularly in Irish ballads as a place of banishment for our freedom fighters. Transportation to that remote outpost of the British Empire was usually permanent and few ever returned. To my young ears, Van Diemen sounded a lot like demon, making it a kind of hell on earth where the vengeful British authorities sent those who dared defy them.

I arrived in Hobart on a direct flight from Melbourne. Hobart is a small city, nestled among the hills flanking the Derwent River before it empties into the Tasman Sea. After Sydney, it's also the second oldest city in Australia.

I checked into a hostel to plan my week in Tasmania. After opening the door to my dorm room, I noticed biscuit crumbs littered across the floor as if a child had been eating there. Shortly after, a thin, balding man wearing thick glasses came into the room and sat on his bed. He continued munching his way through a pack of biscuits, leaving half of them on the floor.

'So, what are you doing in Tasmania', I asked him. His eyes darted around the empty room, checking to see if anyone else was listening.

'I'm studying the effects of nuclear war on humanity. Doing some research in Hobart'.

I smiled evenly, hoping that he wouldn't say any more.

'Do you know there's a nuclear war coming?' he asked me. 'Well, there is. The only place on earth safe enough from attack will be Antarctica. We're currently building bunkers there.'

He bit into a biscuit as he finished his words and chomped loudly, scattering crumbs all over himself and the floor. He didn't seem to notice the mess he was creating. I turned in and tried to sleep as best as I could, considering nuclear war was immient.

Early the next morning, I caught a local bus to Mornington, on the outskirts of Hobart. My plan was to spend the week hitchhiking around the island. My first destination was the former convict settlement of

Port Arthur, only an hour from the capital. I had been a successful hitchhiker during my college years in Ireland and hoped Tasmania would show me the same kindness. I tried to remember all the tricks I used to get a lift. I left my rucksack slightly out of view, faced the oncoming traffic and gave every car the biggest smile I could flash. That wasn't designed to impress the ladies (women generally don't pick up hitchhikers) but to convince drivers I might be an interesting travel companion for part of their journey.

I must have lost some of my hitchhiking mojo because I had to wait an hour before I got my first lift. I struggled with my rucksack as I piled into an old Ford Estate, the engine coughing badly as we took off. I thanked the driver, but he didn't take his eyes off the road, only asking rapid questions. Where are you going? Where are you from? How long are you here for? I finally managed to ask where he was heading.

'I'm off to visit the hospital,' he replied flatly. 'I'm battling brain cancer and have had thirty-one operations so far.'

It was only then he turned his head and I noticed a large part of his skull was missing. I didn't realize it was possible to survive with such an injury. A few miles further on, he dropped me off at the side of the road and drove off towards another possible brain operation. My journey didn't seem so daunting after that.

The process repeated itself during the day, I managed to get lifts but only over short distances. I was delighted when I finally got picked up by a driver who offered to drop me off at Port Arthur. Dave told me he was a marine biologist.

'Do you work in Hobart?' I asked.

'Yes, but I'm actually getting ready to head to Antarctica for a week.'

I thought about my weird roommate from the night before. Maybe he wasn't so mad after all.

'So, any bunkers being built down there?', I asked as casually as I could. He paused for a few seconds.

'What kind of bunkers do you mean?' he asked, never taking his eyes off the road.

Shit, I'd said too much. Even asking that question probably meant I'd be put under surveillance. He'd probably debrief his CIA handlers later that afternoon and that's when it would be agreed that something had to be done. A few days later, I'd probably meet an untimely end by falling down a flight of stairs with my hands bound behind my back. It happens.

As we approached Port Arthur, Dave pointed at a wooden house.

'I assume you heard about the massacre that happened here in 1996. It was there that Martin Bryant killed the first two people on the morning of his rampage,' he informed me.

I distinctly remember seeing the news report where a man had shot and killed thirty-five people in Tasmania. It was the first time I'd heard Tasmania mentioned in the news. It seemed so very far away at the time, an almost forgotten part of Australia suddenly brought into focus by a mindless act of violence. At the time, it was amongst the worst ever mass-shootings in the world. Depressingly, terror attacks such as Paris in 2015 have dwarfed it.

I later read more about the massacre on the internet and the details chilled me. Bryant had gone from the local cafe, gift shop, car park, toll booth and service station, killing indiscriminately as he went. He was captured by police and was sentenced to life in prison with no chance of parole. Why had he committed such a terrible crime? He had a slight mental deficiency but also seemed inspired by the massacre at Dunblane in Scotland. It was the casual way he murdered people that haunted me. He was no berserk killer, no murderer who in the heat of rage had committed that dreadful act. He very deliberately ignored people begging for their lives before coldly killing them. I just couldn't understand it.

Some good did come in the aftermath of the atrocity when the prime minister of Australia, Paul Howard, ushered in new laws to restrict ownership of high-powered automatic rifles and pump-action shotguns. If only other countries would react in the same way to mass shootings.

Once I got settled into the hostel near Port Arthur, I hurried to join the historical walking tour. The guide was a tall man sporting an impressive moustache and a full-length trench-coat. He spoke about the beginnings of transportation in Britain, post-industrialization and overcrowded prisons. Law reform also meant that execution was no longer an easy option as punishment. Port Arthur was an extension of the new reformative prison system in England.

Jeremy Bentham, a noted nineteenth-century philosopher and social reformer, stated that prisons like Port Arthur would help in "grinding rogues honest and idle men industrious". He believed that reform along with punishment would veer these men from their wicked ways. This led to the development of the penitentiary system and Port Arthur was modelled after that system.

Based on this new philosophy, Port Arthur had four guiding principles: discipline and punishment, religious and moral instruction, classification and separation, training and education. These were the four pillars the authorities hoped would grind rogues honest.

After the short tour concluded, I was free to explore the grounds. The first building I visited was the Separate Prison. Instead of lashings and savage beatings, prisoners who committed offences in Port Arthur were sent here for long periods of complete isolation. At the time, this was considered the most enlightened method of reforming prisoners. Once a convict entered the Separate Prison, they were only referred to as a number. They wore cloth hoods outside of their cell so other convicts could not identify them. The floors were scattered with rushes and prison guards wore rubber-soled shoes so no sound would be made. The convicts endured total solitude for twenty-three hours a day, only allowed one hour of exercise in the small yard. Even at church, the seats were enclosed by high wooden panels so they could only see the preacher. The isolation drove many insane, thus requiring a lunatic asylum to be built.

I left the building to visit the penitentiary, one of the oldest structures in Port Arthur. As part of the four pillars, basic education was provided two nights a week. For the majority of convicts, this was their first opportunity to better themselves. Convicts also learned trades such as carpentry, brickwork, tannery, and ironworks. The library had over ten thousand volumes of morally uplifting material. Port Arthur also had the first juvenile prison in the British Empire, opened in 1834 where wayward youths could learn a trade.

When Port Arthur closed in 1877, the local community renamed it Carnarvon in an attempt to erase the convict stain. The site was sold and much of the sandstone from the penitentiary was used for buildings in Hobart and the surrounding area.

The following morning, I decided to visit another place of punishment called the Coal Mines, about twenty-five kilometres from Port

Arthur. I needed some exercise and rented a bicycle from the hostel to make the journey. As I cycled, a cold wind whipped off the sea, chilled by the icy fingertips of distant Antarctica. In addition to the wind, the steady drizzle that began shortly after my departure strengthened into a downpour. It was hard to believe I almost suffered sunstroke a few days earlier on the Australian mainland. The change in weather only a few hundred miles south of Melbourne was staggering. I had only gone a few miles when I was cursing my decision to cycle. The chain slipped off the gears every few miles, making the cycle much harder than it needed to be. What is it with me and bicycles? I can't remember one I've rented that didn't fail to lose a chain, get a puncture, break the handlebars or have the saddle fall off and impale me painfully (only kidding about the last one). The wind and driving rain combined to make it a miserable experience. Maybe this slight hardship was appropriate considering where I was going.

Despite the transport problems, the passing countryside was a joy. Tasmania is about the same size as Ireland and the similarities don't end there. The passing green fields were filled with bellowing cows or bleating sheep. Stonewalled farmhouses had mud-splattered tractors in the yards. Along the road, fences were covered with prickly bramble and blackthorn. These were planted during the convict days, acting as a natural barrier to escape.

After nearly two hours, I reached the coal mines.

There was no entrance fee and I was the only one there. As I looked around the abandoned mines, I felt a dark energy around them. I felt uneasy, constantly looking around to see if somebody else was there. Coal was discovered in the area in 1834 and mines opened soon after. It was soon obvious that the laborious task of extracting coal would be ideally suited to "the worst class" of offenders on Port Arthur. At its peak in the 1840s, six hundred prisoners worked at the mines. The conditions there were dark, damp and very dangerous. When the Reverend Henry Phibbs inspected the mine in 1847, he was shocked by what he saw, recalling "such a scene is not to be forgotten."

The return journey to Port Arthur was even harder than before as my legs were tired and the old bicycle was heavy work. I took a break at a sanctuary for Tasmanian devils, the small but ferocious native animals of the island. About four of them lay in their enclosure, not looking the least bit ferocious. Their home was an over-sized concrete kennel with a small yard for them to play in. The ground was strewn with leaves and bits of tree bark. The warden came along and managed to coax one of them over towards me with some food. The devil was a small black creature with sleek hair and a pointed nose. I had expected them to be much bigger given their reputation. Outside of Tasmania, these devils have been made famous by the Disney character, Taz the Tasmanian Devil.

While the Tasmanian devils survived, the Tasmanian tigers were not so lucky. The tiger looked like a hyena with black stripes down its side. It was once plentiful throughout the island and on the Australian mainland. Deemed a threat to livestock, they were hunted mercilessly until the last one died in Hobart Zoo in 1936. There have been unconfirmed sightings of the creature throughout the island ever since. However, no real evidence has ever been found and the Tasmanian tiger seems to have gone the way of the dodo.

A fter enjoying the history of Port Arthur, it was time to try my luck hitching up the east coast. My first lift of the day dropped me at Eaglehawk Neck. This is a narrow strip of land connecting the Tasman peninsula to the mainland. In penal times, the isthmus was guarded by a line of vicious dogs who impressed one reporter to record, "every four-footed black-fanged individual among them would have taken first prize in his own class for ugliness and ferocity at any show."

Eaglehawk Neck was also the scene of a number of ingenious if ultimately failed escape attempts. One convict named Billy Hunt tried to escape by disguising himself as a kangaroo and hopping across the narrow isthmus. The hungry soldiers on duty saw the creature and started firing at it, only for the kangaroo to shout, 'Don't shoot me, it's only Billy.' On another occasion, convicts tried to avoid the soldiers by swimming across the water with seaweed covering their heads. An alert guard noticed the strange movement of the seaweed in the opposite direction to the tide and they were apprehended.

After waiting for over two hours, a truck driver took me as far as Sorel, roughly twenty miles from Port Arthur. At the rate I was going, I'd never see the island. I made the decision to head back to Hobart and rent a car. I switched to the other side of the road and stuck out my thumb. Luckily, my next lift was a teacher who drove me all the way back to Hobart and dropped me at a car rental depot he recommended. There, I rented a Ford Falcon station wagon for thirty-three bucks a day and I was off again, speeding up the east coast of Tasmania.

With my new wheels, I soon reached Cole's Bay and pulled into the nearby youth hostel. I was tired after the day of hitchhiking and driving and was looking forward to a nice bed for the night with a few beers.

'Sorry mate, no room here tonight,' I was told by a guy at the reception when I asked for a bed. 'A hiking club has taken over the whole place,' he said, jabbing his thumb over his shoulder to a raucous noise coming from the kitchen. I inquired about any other hostels in the area and he sadly informed me there were none. I was crestfallen, I didn't know where to go at that stage.

'What are you driving?' he inquired.

When I told him, he smiled.

'Tell you what mate,' he said. 'There's a free camping area not far from here. I'll give you some bedding to make yourself more comfortable. You'll have plenty of room in the back of the Falcon.'

A few minutes later, he came out with a light mattress, duvet, and pillow.

'Do you want my passport for insurance,' I asked.

'No need, just drop it back in the morning,' he said while helping me load the bedding into the back of the Falcon. Trusting people indeed.

I followed his directions and found the camping spot. When I got to the entrance, the car headlights picked out a strange obstacle barring my way. In the middle of the earthen track, someone had stuck a spade into the ground. I got out of the car and looked around. At first, I thought it must belong to some local work crew but apart from the spade, no other works were visible. A short way away, I could see people in the camping area.

I removed the spade, placing it on the ground nearby and continued to the campsite, parking next to the other campers. As I got out of the car and said hello, the guys there were laughing.

'You're the first one to pass the spade test,' Peter laughed as he shook my hand and introduced me to the rest of his friends. It turned out they had stuck the spade in the ground just to see who would stop and turn around. Apparently, three cars had refused the hurdle.

'Fancy a beer mate,' asked Peter after I sat down with them.

I readily agreed but only, I insisted, if they could spare one.

'Oh, that's not going to be a problem,' he laughed. He threw the plastic tarp off the back of the truck to reveal roughly twenty slabs of beer, like something being smuggled during prohibition. I knew I was going to enjoy the evening.

Before turning in that night, I spotted a squirrel-like creature darting around the campsite in search of food. Peter came over with a spotlight.

'Possums,' he said as the light picked out the little creature. This one carried her young on her back, making it a very cute scene. They didn't seem to fear us but instead approached cautiously when offered food. I turned in to sleep in the back of my car and it was as comfortable as any hotel bed.

Peter woke me early the next morning to show me some rare black cockatoos that had flown into the campsite during the night. Apparently, they're very expensive and breeders will pay thousands of dollars for a good one. I said goodbye to the friendly lads from Hobart before heading back to the hostel to return the bedding.

After driving to Wineglass Bay, I completed the one-hour walk to the lookout which afforded majestic views of the bay. I saw a sign pointing to a trail up Mount Amos, the peak overlooking the bay. I felt adventurous and decided to give it a go. Initially, the going was easy but nearer the top, it got very steep. A strong wind whipped at me as I struggled to hold onto the mountain. I finally reached the summit and drank in the sweeping view of the bay, fringed with white sandy beaches and dense woods along its entire length.

Back at the car park, I spotted a kangaroo carrying a baby in its pouch. Now, I know this is probably a common sight for Australians but for me, it was one of the very things I wanted to see on my visit to the country.

My next stop was Cradle Mountain-Lake St Clair National Park, with its ancient rainforests and alpine terrain. It is home to the world-famous Overland Track and iconic Cradle Mountain, part of the Tasmanian Wilderness World Heritage Area. It was a long drive and the weather was dismal as rain poured from the heavens and the car wipers struggled to clear the windscreen.

Once I got there, I made my way to the Lake St Clair Visitor Center, a lovely wooden building with a roaring fire that reminded me of an alpine ski lodge. Even walking from the car, I got drenched and had to dry myself before the fire. I was relieved to discover there were a few short walks around the park where I could get a taste of the wilderness. Despite the conditions outside, I was determined to get a hike in and opted for the walk around Lake St Clair. Donning my raincoat and boots, I took a deep breath and headed outside.

After five minutes, I stopped walking and wondered what was the point? Rain clouds obscured any visibility and my walk had turned into an exercise in getting wet. Suddenly, the rain stopped and the clouds magically lifted to reveal the spectacular Cradle Mountain. Heartened, I headed off to complete the two-hour circuit of the lake.

With my hike complete, I drove to Strahan on the west coast that evening. I checked into a hostel and booked a cruise for the following day to the infamous Sarah Island. The Island is part of the Wilderness World Heritage Area and the convict site forms one of Tasmania's biggest visitor attractions.

The following morning, I boarded the cruise ship and we sailed up the Gordon River. The ship negotiated the treacherous entry into Macquarie Harbour, which the convicts dubbed Hell's Gate. Further up the river, the forests on either side become denser. It is said to be some of the thickest, most impenetrable woods in the world, much of it unexplored. This was one of the reasons the area was chosen as a convict settlement as there was no escape overland. Much of the forest is made up of "horizontal scrub", trees that grow to form a tangled mess of branches making any progress almost impossible.

After landing on Sarah Island, I joined a very interesting tour of the former convict settlement. Of the one hundred convict deaths there from 1821-33, only thirty-five were from natural causes. Even with such forbidding surroundings, over a hundred prisoners escaped from the island, with seventy more dying in the unforgiving wilderness or murdered by their comrades. A bit more on those escapes soon.

Overgrown ruins were all that remained of the administration building, bakehouse, tannery, and isolation cells. In penal times, towering walls of Huon pine separated civilians from convicts and also acted as a shield against the biting winds that battered the tiny island.

The Island could produce little food and so malnutrition, dysentery, and scurvy were often rampant among the convict population. The penal colony had to be supplied by sea. Living conditions were particularly bad in the early years of the settlement where it was so crowded, convicts were unable to sleep on their backs in the communal barracks. Punishment involved solitary confinement and regular floggings — a total of 9,100 lashes were administered in 1823. I also saw the remains of the old shipyards, one of the largest shipbuilding sites of the British colonies. A plentiful supply of Huon pine made that possible. The penal colony was finally closed in late 1833 and most of the remaining convicts were then relocated to Port Arthur.

'That must have been where *the Frederick* was built,' I overheard a middle-aged couple saying as I took a photo of the old shipyards.

I was intrigued and asked them about it.

'*The Frederick* was the last ship to be built on Sarah

Island,' said Robert, a retired schoolteacher from London. 'Once it was ready, it was fitted out with a crew of ten convicts and sailed back to Hobart. But those boys had other ideas, oh yes they did,' he said, laughing so hard I thought he was going to choke.

'Take it easy Robert,' said his wife, patting his back in a way that suggested she did this quite a lot.

'Anyway,' Robert continued, 'Instead of sailing to Hobart, the convicts took over the ship and sailed it across the Pacific to Chile. In time, four of them were arrested and brought back to Hobart to be tried for mutiny, a crime punishable by hanging. However, at the trial, the men argued that since *The Frederick* had never been registered as a ship, it was in fact only a floating heap of wood. Also, since they hadn't taken over the floating heap of timber on the high seas, they hadn't committed mutiny. The plan worked and they were saved from the gallows.'

Despite its isolated location, a considerable number of convicts attempted to escape from the island. Matthew Brady was among a party that successfully escaped to Hobart in 1824 after tying up their overseer and seizing a boat. James Goodwin was pardoned after his 1828 escape and was subsequently employed to make official surveys of the wilderness he had passed through.

The escape story of Alexander Pearce is probably the best known. Pearce was an Irish convict who, along with other convicts, escaped Sarah Island only to be recaptured shortly after. When quizzed on the whereabouts of his fellow escapees, he admitted having killed and eaten them. His initial confessions of cannibalism were dismissed. He managed to escape a second time with two others and as before, was recaptured. This time however, the human body parts found in his pocket proved his gory claims. Pearce was executed in 1824 – a gruesome end for a man who was sent to Australia for stealing six pairs of shoes.

Much of the brutal reputation of Van Diemen's Land was thanks to the novel *For The Term of his Natural Life* by Manning Clark. Published in 1872, it depicted the brutal convict life on Sarah Island where murder and suicide were common. Beatings, floggings, and violence were the order of the day. Despite being a work of fiction, those savage images burned into the imagination of the public and have been associated with penal Tasmania ever since.

Our final stop of the day was at the Heritage Landing, where I got a chance to walk through some temperate rainforest and learn about the amazing Huon Pine. Visitors flock to see the primaeval forests of myrtle, leatherwood and a species of native pine found only in Tasmania. A raised timber walkway led us through the damp forest to a fallen giant, a two-thousand-year-old Huon pine that continues to support new life in the form of saplings.

'Imagine a bunch of convicts trying to get through that,' a man next to me said, shaking his head in amazement. 'They wouldn't have a bloody chance.'

I had to agree. The dense knot of branches grew horizontally rather than upwards and was entwined with greenery to form a natural wall. I could easily imagine a small family of Tasmanian tigers living in the impenetrable denseness of the woods. Most of the forest has never felt a human touch and would be a perfect hiding place. I can only dream.

A fter returning to Strahan, I got back on the road and drove south towards Queenstown. The views would have been great had they not destroyed all the trees during the mining boom. The surrounding cliffs were stained green and orange by the copper deposits. Heaps of black slag remained from the smelting days. It reminded me of a First World War battlefield where shelling had destroyed every tree, leaving only splintered stumps protruding from the ground. The trees were cut to fuel the copper smelter and the rising toxic fumes killed off the rest of the vegetation. God only knows the effect it had on the people of the area.

It poured from the heavens, but I was determined to make Hobart that night. I was also running low on fuel and relieved that a filling station let me fuel up even though they were closed. I reached Hobart late that night and booked into the same hostel I'd been the previous week. Incredibly, the weird roommate was still there, sprinkling biscuit crumbs across the floor. I saluted him but he didn't seem to remember me.

"You know, there's a war coming," he said, eyes darting about the empty room. I sighed and resigned myself to a fitful night's sleep.

12

MELBOURNE AND SYDNEY

After returning to Melbourne, I discovered my Irish friends James and Lorraine were visiting the city at the same time. I'd met them while living in Boston and couldn't wait to see them again. I took a tram into the city centre to meet them. Melbourne's trams are wonderful, giving the city a very European feel. No matter where you are, you are bound to encounter one of those rattling machines. The trams themselves range from ultra-modern to stock built in the 1940s. There's even a free tram that circles the central business district (CBD), utilizing some old green rolling stock with panelled interiors.

I'd arranged to meet my friends in an Irish pub called PJ O'Brien's. We spent a few happy hours catching up and telling old stories, each one even more embellished than the previous telling.

'Lads, the barman told me there's a huge casino nearby, fancy checking it out after?' said James as he landed three pints of beer on the table without spilling a drop. This is a skill learned over years of dedication, but true mastery is carrying four pints through a packed bar without spilling any beer. If you're good, you can anticipate when people are going to move into your path or when to turn your back to a boisterous group. James was a master of this craft.

The Crown Casino is the largest in the southern hemisphere, a gigantic complex with a wide range of entertainment options on each of its multiple levels. It felt very upscale with lush carpets, coloured lights and mirrors everywhere. We found a few roulette tables where we lost some money but mainly drank and laughed well into the early morning.

I'll be honest, I didn't leave my dorm until lunchtime the next day. I had a fuzzy recollection of agreeing to meet James at Melbourne Gaol, so I called him. Some stranger with a voice like sandpaper answered the phone.

'Hello,' the voice rasped.

'James, John here, how're you feeling,' I said, shocked at the unfamiliar sound of my own voice, like speaking with a throatful of cough syrup.

'Dying,' he replied.

'Me too.'

'Did you say something about Melbourne Gaol?'

'Did I? Like, today?'

'Only if you feel up to it.' This was a direct

challenge to him, was he more hungover than me? After a pause, the line crackled again.

'See you in the hotel lobby in half an hour.'

The rain came down steadily after leaving the hotel and we were relieved to find Old Melbourne Gaol and dryness. The jail is built like a fortress with stout walls and heavy doors studded with huge iron bolts. The heavy timber and iron doors guarding each tiny cell must have made a terrifying sound as they were slammed shut, reminding every prisoner where they were. The main attraction in the gaol concerned one of the most famous Australians of all, Ned Kelly.

Between 1878 and 1879, Ned Kelly operated as an outlaw who hid in the wild Australian bush. Born to poor Irish immigrants, his gang raided and killed for two years. Despite this, they were admired by many who felt they treated the poor well. The gang were finally surrounded by police in a small hotel in 1879 and all except Ned Kelly killed.

'John, look at this,' James said, pointing to a glass case housing the famous iron armour that Ned wore on his final stand against the authorities. Fashioned from ploughshares, the ingenious piece of work protected his head and torso but was ultimately flawed as the police simply shot at his unprotected legs.

After his capture, Ned was brought to Melbourne

where he was tried and sentenced to death. Despite petitions from thousands of people for clemency, he was hanged in Melbourne Gaol on November 11, 1880.

In addition to his fame as a bushranger, Ned also had a way with words. He wrote many letters to the authorities while on the run, one of which contains possibly the best insult ever written. He called the police "a parcel of big ugly fat-necked wombat headed, big-bellied, magpie legged, narrow hipped, splaw-footed sons of Irish bailiffs or English landlords." I smiled as I imagined Kelly and his gang composing the letter in their bush hideout.

In the end, it was his fellow Irishmen who brought him down. He killed an Irish policeman, was captured by one and the hanging judge was a graduate from Trinity College in Dublin. "Such is life," are reputed to have been his last words before he dropped through the gallows floor.

I was aware that my time in Australia was coming to an end and my visa would expire in a few days. I had so much more to see and do but time was against me. That night, I had a lovely meal with James and Lorraine before preparing for the final stop of my Australian adventure.

∾

I arrived in Sydney after yet another epic twelve-hour bus ride from Melbourne. I booked a hostel in the King's Cross area of the city. I was so tired after the bus journey, I slept for the rest of the evening. I woke the following morning and felt annoyed with myself for having wasted some precious exploring time. I only had one day to see the city before catching a flight to New Zealand. It wouldn't be enough to do justice to one of the great cities of the world, but I would have to make do. With no time to waste, I made for the city's most iconic attraction, the Sydney Opera House.

Apart from Uluru, the Sydney Opera House is probably the most recognisable symbol of Australia. No other building in the world is designed in this way, like billowing sails or stacked slices of orange. The building was designed by a Danish architect named Jorn Ulzon in 1957. Ulzon had a radical design calling for a grouping of shells each to be cut from the same sphere, each shell pre-cast of concrete and assembled like a giant Lego set. Despite the reservations of many architects, who considered the design impossible to implement, construction began in the late 1950s. However, the project was so beset by problems, bickering and design changes that Ulzon resigned and went back to Denmark – never to see his dream a reality. A new team of architects completed the work and The Sydney Opera House officially opened in 1975.

After lunch, I walked across another Sydney icon, the Harbour Bridge. Known lovingly as "the coat hanger" by locals, this beautiful suspension bridge connects the business district to the North Shore. Many people do the Bridge Climb where they walk up the bridge supports but I opted not to. The actor Paul Hogan, made famous in *Crocodile Dundee*, was a painter on the bridge before finding his love of acting and hitting it big.

From nearby Circular Quay, I caught a ferry across the stunning harbour towards Watsons Bay. Circular Quay is the major transportation hub of the city, drawing in both locals and tourists before dispersing them to various points of the harbour. From Watsons Bay, I caught a bus to Bondi Beach. In Ireland, newspapers annually feature photos of Irish emigrants enjoying Christmas Day at Bondi Beach. While young people sporting Santa hats and speedos frolicked in the surf, at home we battened down the hatches for yet another rainstorm. I wanted to walk the beach and ogle some bathing beauties in the process. However, Bondi was not what I expected. The beach was almost deserted as a strong wind whipped off the choppy sea. I walked along the beach but soon retreated as so much sand flew into my eyes. Not a beach beauty to be seen in the whole place so I left almost as soon as I had arrived.

However, the return ferry ride back to Circular Quay almost made up for it. The sight of the Harbour

Bridge and Opera House bathed in the setting sun made me yearn to have more time in Sydney.

Returning to my accommodation in King's Cross, I reflected on my day in Sydney. I expected to enjoy the city more but for some reason, I didn't. No question, it's a lovely city with a stunning location on one of the world's great harbours. I found myself walking along one of the busy streets, surrounded by people rushing and talking into their mobile phones. I could have been in any major city in the world. I realized that the city life of Australia was not what I was after. Melbourne and Perth had left me with the same sense of familiar cityscape. I missed the wide-open spaces of Western Australia. I missed seeing kangaroos bounding by the roadside. I missed the stunning sunsets, so beautiful they made me stop in my tracks. I missed the wild adventure of the Outback, with its hardy but friendly people. I missed fishing for barramundi or camping out in the open with the utterly majestic stars of the southern sky above me. Sydney Opera House or the Harbour Bridge did not come close to any of that. I felt I had seen the Australia of my imagination and was satisfied.

I decided to have supper in a bar on the way back to my hostel. As I tucked into a steak, I struck up a conversation with the barman. I told him I was from Ireland.

"Really? My people are from Ireland, they go way back mate," he said as he dried some glasses.

"Do you know what part of Ireland?" I asked.

"Not really, long time ago mate," he replied. "The family say Tipperary but I'm not sure. That's where my family name is from, the O'Dwyers."

I looked at him with a stunned expression.

"No way, that's where my people came from too," I said. "My name is John Dwyer."

"Small world mate," he smiled.

I looked at him. Maybe, just maybe, there was some distant relationship between the two of us. Two distant cousins brought up worlds apart but now only separated by a bar counter.

"You'd never know mate, maybe we're related," he laughed. "You'd never know."

He looked at my near-empty glass.

"Ready for another one mate?" he asked.

"I sure am," I said before draining the last of my beer.

My journey ended when it had begun, downing cold beers in a friendly bar. Not a bad way to end my Outback Odyssey.

THANKS

Thank you for taking the time to read my book, I sincerely hope you enjoyed it. If you did, please leave a review on whatever platform you purchased the book.

I'd love to hear from you so please stop by at johndwyerbooks.com and drop me a line or post a reply to my blog posts. If you signup for my newsletter, you'll be the first to hear about my next book and my writing plans - I promise you, I have some very exciting projects in the pipeline.

Best Wishes,

John

ALSO BY JOHN DWYER

High Road to Tibet: Travels in China, Tibet, Nepal and India

"John Dwyer might be just the ticket to fill Michael Palin's well worn shoes" - HungryFeet.com

Cape Town to Kruger: Travels in South Africa and Swaziland

"A rip-roaring travelogue with real heart" - best-selling author Jeff Gordon

Klondike House: Memories of an Irish Country Childhood

"The author has the wonderful ability to engage the reader and draw them into the past alongside him" - Evening Echo

PHOTOS

(MORE PHOTOS AVAILABLE ON JOHNDWYERBOOKS.COM)

Lying on the statue of a Giant Crocodile, Western Australia

Dominic jumping at Karijini National Park,
Western Australia

*Returning from the canoe trip on Ord River,
Western Australia*

Frill-neck lizard at Kakadu National Park

Giant Termite mound, Kakadu National Park

Gang at Kakadu National Park

Aboriginal rock art, Arnhem Land

Dogs at Eaglehawk Neck, Tasmania

Fremantle Prison, Perth

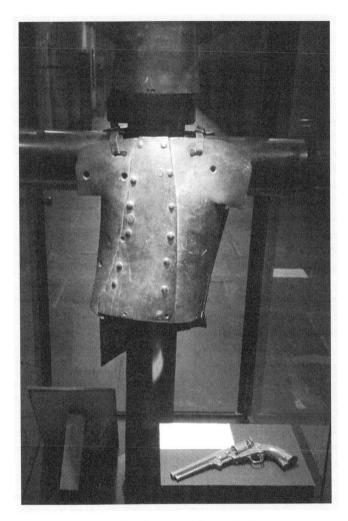

Ned Kelly's amour, Melbourne Gaol

ACKNOWLEDGMENTS

I'd like to thank the following people for their help in making this book possible. Ger Harrington, Noel Phylan, Ger O'Dea, Kieran Harrington and Stephen Meehan.

A special thanks goes yet again to Sarah Lovell who reviewed every chapter and gave me her usual list of positive reviews. She helped make this manuscript so much better.

Any errors are entirely my own.

ABOUT THE AUTHOR

John Dwyer hails from West Cork, Ireland. He suffers from incurable wanderlust and has indulged it in Africa, Asia, Europe and anywhere else that will let him in.

He lives in East Cork, Ireland and continue to churn out his musings on JohnDwyerBooks.com

Printed in Great Britain
by Amazon